BLACKMAN REDEM

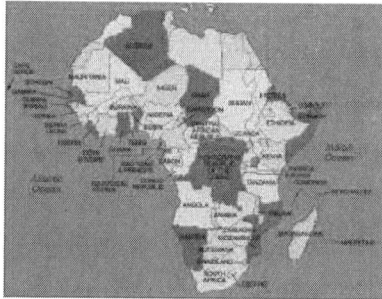

The days are long
Cold
Confusion sets in
Tomorrow comes
Many of the youths of the world have no hope
No home to go
No chance to save themselves

Death comes
Take hold
Lay their claim
A new day is dawn
Evil is all gone

A new beginning comes
A new future
The youths that death did not claim will now find a home
Have a home
They were the ones to adhere to the law and laws of God – Good God
And now they are saved for all eternity

Yes a new day has come
A new song will be sung
True life begins
Void of all ills
Evil
Michelle Jean

Wow, because I truly do not know where to begin. My thoughts are all over the place but I guess that's me. Mind not settled and never will be settled. Too much to think about and write; too much to say.

Been dreaming about youths, young boys as of late hence the title of this book.

I truly do not know why but I guess they too need to be addressed. They too need a talking to as well as need a saving grace. As youths, boys and girls they cannot continue on the pathway of destruction. As things wind down in this evil system of things, they need to know where they stand because hundreds of millions of them will be left without a home, food to eat and water to drink. This harvest is not just for adults it's for them also. They too will find it hard to survive and that's a crying shame. All those that will need medicine will not find any, they will die and we as adults will be at fault.

We are the ones that cannot live good and or well with our neighbours; each other.

We are the ones that cannot respect the boundaries of others.

We are the ones to send our own to fight wars that we truly know nothing about.

Wars that truly do not concern us.

We are the ones to neglect the law and laws of him Good God and Allelujah and because of this, we cannot pay our debts hence death comes to take us including our children – own.

We made our children sacrifices unto death hence many lands will become extinct just like man shortly. Hence I must talk to the children and let them over stand and understand the implications of what is to come and or happen shortly.

They need to listen to good council and heed the voice and cry; words of Good God and Allelujah. They cannot continue on the pathway of death like their parents. If they don't listen, they too will die. And there are no ands ifs or buts about this. This is every human beings reality shortly.

Dreamt I was at a funeral but I could not tell you whose funeral it is. But the funeral was huge; lots of people, black people – males. I cannot fully tell you how the funeral went because all I remember were this group of about 3 Babylonians. But more people were around them. I cannot remember what he, this Babylonian (Indian) boy said to me but he touched me, put his feet on me. People mi grab hold of im foot an tun it up, meaning tun it up in di air a bruk im foot. No im damn feisty a cum put him dutty foot with shoe pan mi like mi an im a quabs – size. Trust me I was mad hence the bruk mi dida bruk im foot.

**To put your feet and dutty shoes on someone is highly disrespectful people. The person is saying they have no respect for you as well as showing you disrespect. You are lowly to them. Hence try your best to never put our feet with shoes on another human being. And we as Black People, Africans and Caribbean Parents wi affi tap beating wi pickney and dog dem with shoes – dutty shoes. It is highly disrespectful and unlawful in the eyes and sight of God – Good God and Allelujah including Man.**

Yes I know the Babylonians are not going to like me because of what is written in the book Instructions for Death but I do not give a rat's ass. The truth had to be told and whether we like it or not, we have to accept our nasty history and sins, traditions and beliefs.

Like I've said, no race on the planet lives for life and or him Good God and Allelujah. We live for death; the Babylonian Way of Life. We were to avoid this sinful and wicked system at all cost because of the different gods they worship; the lies that they tell and the sinful things that they do. Hence I've told you, if the lie (sin) did not work for Eve (Evening), how is it going to work for you? Now I ask you again in a different way, if the lie (sin) did not work for Eve (Evening), how is the Jesus lie going to work for you? I cannot save you if I don't truly know you. He Good God cannot save you if you are not of life – his life. He cannot interfere with nor can he save the devil's own. The devil's children and or death's children and people pree death not life hence they kill daily. *Yes good and evil call on the Breath of Life – Allelujah and or Allah for short but it's not all that will find a home with Allelujah (Allah) because we're not all his own like I've said.* Hence he (Good God) cannot interfere with death and his people. He Good God and Allelujah must leave them alone no matter how much they cry out Allelujah and or Allah to him. You cannot kill and do all that is wrong and say God and or Allah and or Allelujah come on now. You are not saying Good God and Allelujah; you are saying death and crying out to death. Hence they, the children and people of death kill mentally, physically and spiritually. They preach death and sell death. (Religion). And if you are not a part of their wicked and evil system, they do all to destroy and kill you. And it matters not if that destruction is through war or economic means – their financial gain.

As humans we do not truly listen to the word and plea of Good God. We would rather die and go to hell whilst expecting someone to sacrifice self (their life) to save us when we of ourselves can save self. If I know I can save me, I am going to do all to save me. I'm not going to wait on you because at the end of the day, you may never come. You may never show up so why should I or would I wait in vain and lose my place with Good God and Allelujah waiting for you? Good God never told us to wait on anyone, so why wait? Truly help you because you know your sins not the next person if you do not tell them. Come on now.

I did my wrongs hence I have to correct them and do better for self, you, my family and Good God himself. You did not do my wrongs and or sin for me, so why should I expect you to pay and or correct them for me? It's like saying, *"Mr. Bank Manager, I know I have a mortgage but watch ya man, mi naah pay yu because sey di man dung di road ago pay di mortgage fi mi."*

"Who's the man down the road that is going to do this?' Replied the Bank Manager. 'Call him because you're 6 months in arrears and you just got this mortgage. The bank needs to be paid."

"But Sa, you noa di man."

"I know di man," the bank manager looked at him weird and suspiciously. He could not believe this man could say such a thing. He didn't even know the man nor did he know what he was talking about.

"Yes, im name Jesus and im ago pay mi mortgage."

"Sir, how is Jesus going to pay your mortgage? It is not Jesus who owes the bank but you."

"But Sar Jesus said, he died so all would be saved."

"And you are forgetting that not all in humanity believe in your Jesus. I don't believe in him because I am not of his belief system. So how are you going to pay the bank the money that you owe them?"

"Di bank just going to have to wait." He said bold faced with a smile. He was a devoted Christian that put all his faith and trust in Jesus and the belief system of Jesus. He could never be wrong because he trust Jesus to supply all his needs including pay his mortgage, debt. He said all that believed in him would have everlasting life and he had to believe this at all cost. He could not stray not even with what the Bank Manager said. Jesus was his money in the bank to get him through and he could not be rocked; this was his faith and it was his faith until the end.

"Sir, Mr. Anderson, the bank cannot wait any longer. You signed a contract stating you can pay your mortgage. You provided us with all the necessary information and we trusted you to pay your debt and or obligation to us on time. Now here you are telling us you cannot pay. Someone else is going to pay for you!" The Bank Manager said angrily. He could not believe someone would be so daft; stupid. He could not believe the ignorance of this man. He owed the bank but yet he is expecting someone else to pay his debt for him instead of securing himself – his future.

"You gave us your word that you would not default on your loan and here you are defaulting. We gave you enough time to come up with the money and now you're telling us Jesus is going to pay. You cannot produce this Jesus with our money so we have no other option but to foreclose."

"You can't foreclose. I own this house, Jesus owns this house."

"No, the bank owns your house and all that is in it including the land your house is built on. Your appliances, the bank owns. Your television and stereo the bank owns. Your clothes and shoes including car the bank owns. You and your family the bank owns because we are going to garnish your wages and collect every cent including interest and legal fees that belongs to us if we do not get what is rightfully due to us."

"But Jesus won't let you."

"Jesus cannot stop us because Jesus' signature in not on your bank note; loan, yours is."

"But you can't do this."

"We can and did. When you neglect to pay your loan, you gave us all rights to do this. You have an obligation to the bank and you neglected your obligation and when you do this, we can do whatever we want. As we speak the locks to the house is being changed. Your car that is sitting outside has been repossessed. The only thing you have to your name is the clothes on your back. Good day Mr. Anderson. It was a pleasure doing business with you."

"But what about my family?"

"Tell it to your Jesus. I am sure he can do more to help you."

"But"

"You've lost everything."

"Yes"

"Well that is something you should take up with your Jesus. Because he was obviously not working for you and or in your behalf."

"But you."

"I am not you sir. I pay my mortgage. I do not depend on others to do it for me. We've all been told God helps those who help themselves. So if you don't pay your bills how do you expect your bills to be paid? If you do not put forth the effort to help you and your family, how are they going to eat; live?"

"But Jesus."

"Never said, he was going to pay your bills for you. You incurred your debt; you are to clear them up because they are your responsibility. Jesus did not put you in debt, you put yourself in debt so why should he pay your debt for you?"

"Sir, I am sorry I need time."

"You've ran out of time. ALL THE VOICE MESSAGES, TEXT MESSAGES AND LETTERS WE SENT YOU, YOU IGNORED. I'm sorry I cannot extend your time because you ignored your calling and now it is truly too late."

"Sar mi beg yu. Mi no ha nowhere to go," dropping to the floor and pleading with the Bank Manager for mercy.

"And that is not my fault but yours. We all have our jobs to do Mr. Anderson and we've given you time to get your life and finances in order. Instead of doing so, you neglected

us and squandered our time, your time. So no I will not extend your time."

"Sir mi family."

"You should have thought of them before you neglected your responsibilities. Go day Mr. Anderson."

"Du sar." Pleading; begging the Bank Manger for mercy, lenience but none was given to him because he was truly too late. He ignored his warning letters, phone calls and text messages the bank sent him in regards to his loan. He thought someone else would pay his debt hence he waited on faith; his faith and his faith failed him. All that he could do to help himself he did not do and now it's truly too late because whether he knows it or not, his Jesus did not put him in debt, he did that all on his own. His Jesus' signature was not on the bank note; loan his was and his alone so how could he expect his Jesus to pay his debt when he Jesus did not make them? Nor did he Jesus come to his rescue and tell the Bank Manager he knew Mr. Anderson and he would secure his payment so that he did not default on his loan.

"Security, please come and get this man out of my office." And so the deed was done. Mr. Anderson sealed his faith and lost it all instead of truly helping himself.

Life isn't easy and we all know this hence we need to focus on the youths of today. As parents we can no longer mess them up with religious bullshit because

religion is from hell and not from Good God and Allelujah. Religion does not speak the truth hence the clergy lie to us each and every day. This is why I will forever ask, what religion is Good God and Allelujah? We all claim to have him but fail to understand and comprehend we all have death. We do not have him because all we are taught is death, how to die and go to hell. Religion does not teach us how to live because if it did so much war and strife would not be on land – earth. We would not hate each other and put enmity between each other.

We are to tell the truth but evil cannot stand the truth because evil do not want to lose their place with their father; death.

- ❖ *See when evil stop, the hatred stops.*
- ❖ *When evil stop, there will be no more religion – religious lies.*
- ❖ *When evil stop, there will be no more enmity between man and God – Good God.*
- ❖ *When evil stop, there will be no more hatred and strife between the races.*
- ❖ *When evil stop, destruction stops.*
- ❖ *When evil stop, death will not come it will stop and life – true life will begin.*

Religion give us death hence we truly do not know how to live. They (the clergy) give us false hope because they say we have to die to see and have life and this is infinitely and indefinitely wrong; a lie. <u>*You have to live to see life because we were told "truth is everlasting life" and without truth we cannot live. We die because lies are sins; have not life but death.*</u> Now I ask you this, if we have not truth, how are we going to live?

We can no longer base our lives on religious beliefs because if religion could save humanity, we would not be slated to die before 2032 and I've told you this.

If religion could save us and was of Good God and Allelujah, we would all be living good and clean and void of all sin and sins.

As humans we would not be breaking the law and laws of Good God and Allelujah, come on now.

Allelujah is life hence we are to call out to him. But yet not one of us can, nor can we respect him. We say we love him but yet show him so much hate and disrespect.

We say we trust him but yet, we call upon death for all our needs.

We say we trust him but yet, we bow down to death and worship death.

We say we trust him but yet, he cannot trust us because we do not have his back nor are we loyal to him. We do not hold him dear to us nor do we hold him in high esteem and regard but yet, we say we are calling on him. You're not calling on him, you're calling on the devil; death. Come on now.

We have to respect God – Good God and respect self because at the end of the day, your life; good and true life is worth it.

We cannot wait on someone to come and save our children because you will be waiting in vain. I am not saying someone won't come and help you but what about those that truly need help? How many years and or decades have they been waiting for help and help does not come? Hence you cannot sit and wait for help. Truly help you in a good and positive way. We all want freedom but refuse to take that one step towards freedom.

We all want to be happy but refuse to get up off the sofa and go for a walk. Yes it's hard for some because the strangle hold and or noose around your neck is hard to pull.

__Hence always remember when your strangle hold is physical it is not so for some. Some are spiritually bound hence their strangle__ *hold is for a lifetime and or until they die and or get released. Some do not get release and or released from these strangle hold (s). There are things called generational curses and or sins and you see this and or read about this in your book of sin – so called holy bible when Noah cursed Canaan. Our sins and or evils can cause a nation of people to get cursed and or left out of Good God's kingdom indefinitely forever ever. And this is what happened to the Babylonians and many Black Nations today. Yes Nations of Islam. As Black Nations we would rather accept the devil's own and their lies told on Good God and Allelujah and condemn self, land and people rather than accept the truth and walk away and or pass over death infinitely and indefinitely forever ever without end.*

Hence you have the many different churches and religions of death; religious faiths and organizations that the black community join and are in globally to kill self. We are not loyal to God – Good God and Allelujah. Nor are we loyal to our own, our history, culture, heritage, truths and beginning. Instead of keeping our true roots – hair, we take on the hair of death and accept their own. Basically what we are telling Good God and Allelujah is that, all that he's given us is not worth it. Not good enough and the culture, hair and ways (sins) of Babylon is better than his.

Physical hell and spiritual hell is not the same hence truly know how you are bound. Our children should be a priority when it comes to raising them right. Hence I will not have Babylonians that are locked out to Good God and Allelujah's abode put their nasty foot on me without retaliating. Do not bring war to me lest I destroy you rude and wicked with my words and the words of Good God and Allelujah. *Time is my right and keep hence evil and wicked people has their time in time when they must die due to their evil and wicked ways. Those of us that truly know Good God and Allelujah know to leave their enemies to time because "WE KNOW THE WAGES AND OR PAY OF SIN IS DEATH." Death must take all wicked and evil; sinful people. We also know the fire of HELL HENCE HELL AWAITS ALL WICKED AND EVIL PEOPLE, THUS SAITH THE LORD THY GOD MEANING IT IS SO.*

Hell is the kingdom and domain of death, hence the fire that consumes the spirit, all wicked and evil spirit in the end; the end of their time on earth; the physical realm is not the same as earthly fire.

These people did not want Good God and Allelujah hence they locked themselves out of his kingdom; good and true abode.

Also, I will not have them telling me how to raise my children because they have no good family values. They use their book of sin – so called holy bible that was written by wicked and evil men to justify their sins – wicked and evil living – ways; wrongs.

They are people of sacrifice and I am not. I refuse to sacrifice my child and or children to death because death is not life, it is death; dead. Why the hell should I give my child and or children over to death when death did not feel the pain to have them?

I truly value all life, wicked and evil people don't, hence they deal in incest and all that is nasty, dirty and unclean. They are not of Good God and Allelujah so why should I be of them and their nasty systems of condemnation and filth. Their god and gods love stench hence they sacrifice each other;

sacrifice their lives for death, accept death and live for death, a place in hell. Their way of life is cursed, so why should I or would I live like the cursed when I can live clean and secure in the realm and home; house of him Good God and Allelujah?

They are not of God because the cow is their god – sacred to them and I've told you the significance of the cow in Instructions for Death. No Babylonian can blame him Good God and Allelujah for their demise because they are damned liars like their father Satan. They do all for death hence they do all to bring you to hell with them.

Like I've said, I respect Good God and Allelujah and at times it's not easy. Many of us falter; cannot stay true because it's not an easy road to walk when spiritual wickedness surrounds you. Physical wickedness we can walk away from but there is no escaping spiritual wickedness for some. Spiritual wickedness does not give up. If you are weak you cannot overcome hence many times I lash out at him Good God for rescue. Sometimes the lashing out seem disrespectful but when you feel this way, stop and talk to him Good God. Tell him how you feel because our hurt and pain is real and at times it is that severe. Truly learn to trust him because he does truly understand what you are going through. Many may not understand but I do not trust many, I truly trust him Good God because he is the healer and fixer of everything. If he tells you to walk away from something take your time and walk away. If he says no not say, he will show you what to do. If he shows you the way then take the way he shows you. Meaning if your way is to leave your job that you are not happy in, find another before you leave your job. Don't just leave your job like that. Make sure you have another one and leave the job that is causing you pain in true peace. Never leave in wrath and anger.

Will he tell you not to be with a particular person? Yes he will so truly learn to rely on him and how he speaks to you. This is why I tell you time and time again to know your colours as in the colour of your clothing. I tell my children not all because some are not of the age of comprehension yet but the oldest ones I tell, if they see a woman descending down upon them (hovering over down on them) to run from that woman like a thief in the night because she is their death in the physical realm. I did not tell them she's their death in the spiritual realm and I will shortly because she's death all around. It's the same thing for my daughter. If she sees a man hovering over her in black then she is to run because that man is her death in the physical and spiritual realm. No one is to hover over you in your sleep people. This is bad hence many of us truly do not know how death comes in the living and the spiritual realm.

Some of us do not know this and I found this out the hard way hence I will teach you how death comes when I see death. Avoid death at all cost because whether you know it or not, if that person dies, say you married that evil person, he or she can take your life when they are dead and some do try.

Meaning some people feel a sense of attachment in the living and in death and if so being that person can and some do take you with them, shortly after they have died. They need you with them so they take you to join them in the spirit world.

Listen, I truly love him Good God and Allelujah and I refuse to let wicked and evil people including spirits take him from me or me from him. He Good God and Allelujah is my right and he's also my choice over death and all that is wicked and evil. If you want to die then die but don't take me with you because I refuse you and death.

DEATH IS A CHOICE NOT A RIGHT. IT IS A CHOICE WE MADE AND MAKE. WE ARE THE ONES THAT CHOSE TO DIE DUE TO OUR SINS – WRONGS. *You cannot choose death and expect to live. You can only die and this is what's*

going to happen to billions shortly if they don't change their dirty linen of self.

As he Good God and Allelujah have his race so does the devil. And like I've said in the Instructions for Death, Good God and Allelujah did not put enmity between his seed and Satan's seed nor did he choose death for anyone of us. We are the ones to choose death and in so doing we also chose death for our children. We were to separate from them (evil's children) and leave them the hell alone but none of us can do this because we think we are all from the human race when we are not. We are not all God's children hence refusing to put two and two together. Peace – true peace is not in the hearts of death's children hence they kill and tell lie on Allelujah (Allah) who is the breath of life. *YOU CANNOT SAY YOU HAVE LIFE – THE BREATH OF LIFE AND KILL. YOU ARE A DAMNED LIAR BECAUSE "THOU SHALT NOT KILL." And life cannot kill it can only live. Grow up in a positive and good way to him Good God and Allelujah. Death kills not life. Come on now.*

You cannot say you have the breath of life and tell lies on the breath of life. Polygamy. Come on now. "Thou shalt not commit adultery." Hence none of us live for life (Good God and Allelujah); we all live for sin – death.

When you do all of this you know not life hence you have no life in the physical and spiritual realm. <u>And this is why revelations say we are the first begotten of the dead.</u>

No Babylonian, not one is found on the Mountain of Good God and Allelujah. Hence none, not one will be saved because they are not of him, they are of the devil. They are of death hence they worship and praise fire, even walk on fire and dance with fire. I will not have compassion for a race of people that have no good will for humanity and Good God and Allelujah including self. I refuse to. Hence I truly do not want any in this knew kingdom. And if this makes me racist so be it because I am looking at the ills, lies and sins of humanity not the colour of skin, race or creed. If a race or nation of people have no good will for me and my God – King – Life – All, why should I want or need you in my kingdom or even have good will towards you? Why should I have compassion and or a saving grace for liars and thieves, wicked and evil people that have no compassion for self or anyone? Stay the bleep out and stay the hell away from me because I truly do not want or need nothing (anything) to do with you or from you. You have no good will for me so why should I have good will towards you when you cause me hurt and pain? Trust me I am going to avoid you like the plague because in my eyes you are condemned. *TRUST ME I WILL NOT HATE YOU. AND I REFUSE TO HATE YOU BUT I WILL NOT CONTAMINATE MYSELF BY BEING IN CONTACT WITH YOU. BESIDES HATING YOU WOULD BE AN INDEFINITE WASTE OF ENERGY, MY GOOD ENERGY AND TIME. Energy and time I could use for doing more positive things in life.* Immigration wise, you can't come to my borders or vacation on my property. And no, I will infinitely and indefinitely not lift up arms against you. Why the hell would I sin myself and land and become condemned by lifting up arms against you? You're not worth it, hence I live for life and try my best to do all the good I can do in life, for life and my GOOD AND CLEAN GOD – GOOD GOD AND ALLELUJAH.

Listen, he Good God and Allelujah is my right and anything negative that I do take him away from me. So because he Good God and Allelujah and me (I) is that tight – closer than close, I aim on keeping him good and true to me in all that I do. I don't want you in my land or lands so stay the hell out because you are not clean. Come on now.

Look at humanity today. All that he Good God and Allelujah tell us not to do we do.

Instead of breaking away from evil and stay true to him Good God and Allelujah, we teach our children in the like manner of sin and death and wonder why some die brutally.

Some of us are the cause of death – the reason why our children die and refuse to see this; change our dirty and unclean ways.

We refuse to learn the truth and when death bax wi dung an a put on di vice grip of death pan wi wi still no learn.

PEOPLE, "OUR SINS WILL CAUSE DEATH TO TAKE OUR CHILDREN BEFORE THEIR TIME." So stop teaching your children wrong and let them live. Come on now.

When we sin death have to collect pay and it matters not if that pay is our children or someone we truly love.

SIN NOT AND DEATH WILL NOT COME AND I'VE TOLD YOU THIS ALREADY IN MY OTHER BOOKS. So take heed because the more we sin is the more we die. Meaning, it's the longer you stay in hell and burn before your eventual death. Your sin and or sins affect the next individual including the land that you live in BECAUSE ALL HAVE LIFE. Hence truly look into yourself and see life, your life and the life of others. It is not right for someone to send you on the battlefield to fight another man's war because he's taking your life away. And it matters not if that battlefield is financial, gang related or pharmaceutical related. And when I say pharmaceutical related, I am talking about you designing and or developing and or creating diseases, biological warfare and weapons including nuclear weapons to kill someone and or nations in humanity. When you do this, you are also taking away from the life of your family and country. Hence many lands (countries) cannot repay their debt to death and I've told you this before. See and or Look at America National Debt load because they are a prime example of this.

Look at my homeland Jamaica as well because they are a prime example of the modern day Sodom and Gomorrah. See they the people of my homeland forgot about Port Royal and the sins and evils that went on there in the 1600 hundreds. Those sins were not repaid hence the interest on that debt (death) have and has skyrocketed (inflation). Hence the deeming of the island dirty – unclean recently by him Good God and Allelujah. And like I've said; my homeland and or people can save themselves. He Good God did give them a life line to save self. But I truly do not trust any of them to become like the people of Nineveh and repent of their sins infinitely and indefinitely forever ever. They are to become 99.9% clean like Lysol in the yellow bottle. It means they are to clean self and land including home. If they don't do this, then they will have nothing left because I've told you time and time again that death wants them. Death wants them so bad that I've stepped aside to let death do his and her will – work.

__You cannot have the name of Good God – Ja in your name and do so much evil that he Good God and Allelujah deemed you dirty – unclean. Come on now. We say we are blessed but everyone has forgotten this blessing because the EAT A FOOD BUSINESS IS STILL PREVALENT ON THE ISLAND.__

❖ *Di Obeah business still prevalent.*

❖ *The I'm better than you attitude still prevalent because some have more education than others. Hence many become snobs and look down on the have nots like dem betta dan anyone. Dem gwaane like dem shit no stink like di next man or woman. Some so stuck up that it's a wonder how stuck up no stamp inna dem forehead fi all to si.*

❖ *Dem so stuck up dat dem figet sey some a dem was damn field slaves before dem get promotion by massa to become woserra fools that the system can manipulate and do manipulate.*

❖ *Dem gwaane like fi dem quatty betta dan fi mi an fi yu quatty because dem live in a betta house and drive a nicer car and have more money in the bank. And with all that said, some still a creep downtown to get true and real loving and or sexual healing. Some gwaane like dem nuh bow but dem a bow cat pro and master because all dem can use a dem tongue and nothing else. Hence dem lap dem fraktail at another man's door begging for more.*

❖ *The why did God choose you over me attitude come into play. Hence the jealousy and di run some run to obeah man and woman, witchcraft workers of the highest order to keep you down as well as keep you from succeeding.*

❖ *The bible and key nastiness come into play.*

❖ *Di parchment paper business comes into play.*

❖ *The sprinkling rum at grave site and chanting and or singing to the dead comes into play.*

❖ *The powda sprinkling at someone's doorstep come into play.*

❖ *The using of pigs (pork) in obeah working comes into play.*

❖ *The burying of bottle – nastiness at someone's gate fi tun dem dung and kill dem comes into play. All this and more including killing – sacrificing others for money and fame our people do to keep others down without realizing that all the evil that they do, affect the true and good, positive prosperity of their lives and land. Hence contributing to the failure of people and country – economic growth and well being.*

Trust me I will not sacrifice the good will of Good God and Allelujah for any. Death is death hence they are the dead and Revelations tell you this.

They (the Babylonians) including billions of you are the first begotten of the dead – death. So if you are dead how can you say life? How can you have life when you are born of dead; death?

As parents we lack good parenting skills. Me too but I try to do the good that I can. As parents sometimes we can talk to our children until we are blue in the face when it comes to good council and conduct and they (our

children) do not listen. It does not mean you are a bad parent because you've done the best and good you can. Hence you should not be ashamed of the wrongs your children do. Remember goodness is not guaranteed when it comes to our children because friends; their peers can affect them in a negative way. You as a parent can be telling them (your children) right and someone else is telling them wrong. So you truly cannot blame yourself. You just have to leave that child to time whilst praying truthfully to Good God and Allelujah that they come out of their predicament if they are in one. Remember children can be rebellious and some are but that is not your fault if you are teaching right – true. And yes I know some parents can be bitches because some teach wrong and encourage their child and or children to do wrong.

Also remember, we baptize and christen our children in sin – death, so expect them to become rebellious and do all for sin and death. LIKE I'VE SAID, WE TEACH WRONG AND EXPECT OUR CHILDREN TO BECOME RIGHT AND THEY CANNOT.

THEY CAN ONLY BECOME WRONG. SO TEACH RIGHT AND LET YOUR CHILD AND OR CHILDREN BECOME RIGHT; JUST AND CLEAN.

Truth is not failure it is life.

Lies are failures hence lies are sins and they cannot be repaid just like that. THE WEIGHT OF LIES AND OR OUR SINS IS GREATER THAN OUR GOOD; ANY GOOD THAT WE DO. SO TRY YOUR BEST NOT TO SIN; DO WRONG.

If you do wrong and or sin beg forgiveness all around and try not to make those sins and or do those sins again. If you wronged a man and or person including Good God and Allelujah, beg forgiveness. If that person and or individual and or company forgives you then great you are in the clear. If no forgiveness is given, make penance and sin offering by going to Good God and Allelujah and tell him that that person and or company did not forgive you and this is what I would like to do. If your like to do is giving $5.00 to a charity or buying $5.00 in groceries and giving it to your neighbour and or food bank do so. But do all you can to make amends. Do not bug the person and or company you asked forgiveness from, go another route. _Tell God – Good God of your intention and let him make your sin records right like I've just said. Meaning that penance and or good that you do goes on your good record as payment in another form. And give for 3 months $5.00 in food because each good that you do has a weight of 10 000. So give until you have wiped out that sin. And the $5.00 is not weekly or bi-weekly it is monthly._ Trust me you will know when that sin is wiped out. And please do not give what you do not have. Your good can be in prayer and or praise and thanks to him Good God and Allelujah. And don't be stingy when you are talking to him because some of us have stingy prayers – talk.

Yu tell dem (your children) nuh run crase di street an dem run crase it. Dem nuh stop crase di street till one day car lick dem dung an you hear how car man wicked; kill mi pickey. We figet sey wi pickney wicked to because he or she never listened to good council. They disobeyed you and now look at the consequences. Hence they too must go down in flames because of disobedience.

Listen, I have the same problem in my house. I tell my children one thing and they don't listen. I see the danger before it happens and I tell them of the danger and still they don't listen. So who no hear shall feel one day. There comes a point in your life as a parent when you are going to get fed up and tired and say, let what happen to dem happen because dem naa listen – hear.

I see the younger generation of today and it's as if they care not for their future. All they care about is the dollar bill and it matters not how they get this money. No I will not paint a pretty picture on this one because some kids are beyond reasoning. Yu tell dem including some a fimi fi gaah school an dem nuh waane guh. They feel dem nuh need fi gaah school and further their education because they won't need it in the future. Listen it's a foolish child that think this way because soon you will need a university degree to clean floors; be a cleaner. The requirements of the workforce will be extreme as jobs become scarce and if you do not have the requirements no one is going to look at your resume.

Hard times is going to be global hence the haves will lose it all real soon and when this happens you will see the trickling effect in the workforce and economy. Governments will not be able to provide for all. *Yes we've adopted the Western Mentality train of thought whilst forgetting where we truly came from.*

Things are not working out for many of you (the Black Race of the West) but yet we refuse to say screw it, Africa here I come and invest in our future there. Yes I know many Blacks are not of African Decent but it does not mean you cannot invest in your future in European Lands. No European country can say Black Man come out of my Land or Country because Europeans are not all Whites. Some are Blacks and we as Blacks not Babylonian Blacks can claim any European Land as our own. But the problem is which land can we claim? We don't even know our ancestry to say this is where my ancestors came from. We all think we are all Africans and in truth we are not all Africans hence we are like trees without roots; have not a home – a true home.

Many have the opportunity to further self they are giving up. You have to be constantly drilling education into their heads and still they are not listening.

You have to be constantly pushing them to excel.

Constantly telling them (our kids) to strife for something better and still they are not listening. *See the limit thinking and limited space bullshit when it comes to being boxed in don't work with me.* The future is there and we are the ones to grab it but yet some of these young brothers are not grabbing it. And some of the ones that do grab it fail miserably because they did not learn nor did they care to learn about their investment options. *Yes life is given but it is also an investment. You have to invest in you in order for you to succeed. You have to make positive choices in order for you to succeed.* As a young brother stop with the Nigger mentality and start thinking like a young man that want positive things for self. Instead of investing 20 – 30 thousand dollars or even 5 000 dollars in a car, invest it in your future; an education. Get your College Diploma or University Degree.

But I don't want to go to College or University I want to do something with my hands. I love energy, electricity and plumbing. Then invest your five thousand dollars in a trade school and get your electrical license and or plumbing degree and or license.

My son has friends that love electricity and would like to be electricians. This is fine but what I tell them is to learn about solar paneling (energy). Specialize. I'm looking into Geo Thermal Energy because somehow I thing Geo Thermal Energy will be the wave of the future and if they can get a head start in this field then do it. Do not be limited in your field of work. Specialize and grow. This is my train of thinking hence I truly do not like the box nor will I let anyone box me in. My brain is constantly thinking hence I truly need to tap into my limitless resources of the brain; mind.

I know not all want to go to College or University but you know what; there are trades out there as well as trade schools that you can go to. You have to be future ready lest you will be left in the dark. My children know what they want. Not all but a couple and like I tell my oldest child. Do not look in one area to find a job. Diversify and look elsewhere including out of province or state. Be opened minded and go outside of the box. Do not let me hinder you from succeeding because at the end of the day, he including you need to live your life and further your education in life when it comes to life. I will never hold any of my children back when it comes to growing and achieving as well as learning. Learn all the good you can as well as know the bad. The bad things you stay away from at all cost because these are the things that will hurt you and even kill you. Hence teach your children good and well so that they have what they need to succeed in the future.

Why is the question I ask? Why do we as parents have to be constantly on our children's back for the betterment of them?

The education system is there no matter how lousy you think it is. Some of you made the choice to drop out of school and follow bad company. So live with the consequences and stop blaming the system. The system said this is all I can offer, accept it or reject it.

Many choose to reject it and drop out. Now some are in jail, some are strung up in hospitals, some are on the system (welfare) and some are strung out on drugs and selling drugs. Yes some are dead too. None of us can blame the system for this. You made the choice so you have to blame you for the bad choices you've made.

- ❖ *You chose not to go to school.*
- ❖ *You chose the folly ground.*
- ❖ *You chose to ignore the right and good choice for you.*
- ❖ *You chose to have children too early.*
- ❖ *You chose to deceive yourself and others; the family that truly loves you.*
- ❖ *You chose not to secure your future and the future of your children. Hence many of you lose it all by buying your way through life. And this includes buying women and showering them with gold, silver, cars, houses, shoes, lingerie. You name it you buy it for them whilst some of your children are starving and living in cardboard and shoe boxes. None of you thought of the future. You just thought of the here and now; self gratification – sins.*

Life became a game to many of you hence you played it foolishly and lost in the end. I truly do not feel sorry for many of you because you made the money and neglected your own including community that you grew up in.

Life isn't a game hence we are to live it good and clean. Education is our right not a choice because knowledge grows and knowledge is one of the keys to life. You did not want it hence you left it alone. So truly stop blaming others for you not having your education and or the finer things you want and need in life.

Stop blaming others because you spent foolishly. You bought friends and hairy motels hence no one in your circle was loyal.

Education is free for many so truly take advantage of it before it's too late.

And to the guidance councillors globally, stop hindering Black Children. Stop telling them they cannot be who they want to be.

If a child want to be a doctor stop telling them that field is not for them. Who the fuck are you to do this? Encourage them and give them the tools and proper information for success. I am so sick of this. The world is big; vast. That child don't have to stay in one geographical area to excel and or work. So stop limiting children especially black children because none of you would like it if we the black race were limiting you. Come on now.

My daughter wants to teach; be a teacher but yet you are telling her the field is filled. Stop this because she doesn't want to stay in the country and teach. She wants to go elsewhere.

As humans we are not limited. We are the ones to make wicked and evil including jealous people limit us and this is sad.

We know right from wrong but yet we choose wrong over right and this is sad.

As young boys and girls you have to stay true to your dreams and let no one hinder you from doing what truly makes you happy. Be passionate about your aim and or goals and take tiny steps in achieving them positively not negatively.

If you want to be a doctor and this is the field you are passionate about. Be a doctor.

If brain surgery is your field of choice, research what you need to do to become a brain surgeon and take tiny steps now to achieve your goal and or dream. Never ever let anyone take you off your path of truth do you hear me. Not even your parents or me.

"I don't have the money to send you to college or university," some parents will say.

<u>**Listen to me and listen carefully and well. There are scholarships, bursaries including student loans and grants out there. Work part – time or get a summer job if you can and save up to help you and your future.**</u> *Every little bit help, so do and get the every little bit to help you.* **REMEMBER THESE EVERY LITTLE BIT WILL NOT COME TO YOU IF YOU SIT AND WAIT BECAUSE FOR SOME THESE EVERY LITTLE BIT DO NOT COME. SO TRULY DO FOR YOU AND HELP YOU.** *Your future is worth it. So truly do not be like the lazy ones that sit and wait for a handout as well as think the system owes them something. The system owes us nothing because the system did not lay with your mother and get you.* <u>***And if you are one to say well look at slavery and what the system did to our forefathers hence I want repatriation. I am going to tell you to screw you because our forefathers did sell us into slavery to the highest bidder. Hence some of our dirty African History is eliminated out of the history books because of shame and disgrace. They***</u>

tell us we are all Africans but we are not all Africans some are Indian (Babylonian), Chinese and White, of Asian and European as well as Babylonian lands and decent.

Do not be like me and let people hinder you. Hence the hindrance have and has stopped. I am taking baby steps towards my happiness. I've let go of spiritual hindrance and taking baby steps towards helping me physically and spiritually.

You have to stay strong and do all the good that you can. Even when you think it is not worth it to do good and or he Good God and Allelujah has and have failed you. You have to continue forward because those negative doors are not for you. I've learned that things take time and it's okay to give up. But when you give up today, regroup for tomorrow and try another route. Keep regrouping until you find the right route. When you do things will be okay.

Never ever forget that all the devil gives you, he will take it back eventually. You must lose it all; go bankrupt and trust me when this happens you will never gain it all again.

Trust me he will have you strung out on:
- ❖ *Drugs*
- ❖ *Alcohol*

- ❖ *Sex*
- ❖ *Gambling*
- ❖ *Adultery*
- ❖ *Prostitution*
- ❖ *All that is sinful*

And I've told you this before in another book. So be on your guard because evil – wicked and evil people including spirits will seek your fall – downfall.

You the youths of today are the future generation. No, that's not true because many of you are not living true. Many of you your parents sold you out to the devil literally. And yes that sellout includes religion.

Many of you are ill willed hence the gun and violence is your game and name to fame. Instead of securing your future you would rather screw it up rather than move on. Shit happens in life that you cannot control and you have to learn this. Stop looking for a place to belong hence the folly and or bad ground you choose is your choice and your choice alone. Why cut your life short for the next man and or person? Life isn't about pain it's about growth; positive growth and you have to learn this.

"Well my daddy walked out on my Mama."

And your point? The relationship your mother had with your father has nothing to do with you; it has to do with him and her. Learn from their mistakes and don't make the same ones they make when you are older.

Mommy and Daddy's relationship is mommy's and daddy's. They chose each other hence they have to live with their lies. Neither found lifetime partners hence the lies they tell to each other each and every day.

Neither were honest hence the commitment was not honest. And yes one can be honest whilst the other is not hence the relationship failed. One parent can't be tugging this way whilst the other tug the other way. It will not work and eventually the relationship will crash and burn; end in divorce.

Your parent's divorce had nothing to do with you; it had to do with them. How they conduct their lives after the split is also up to them. Some choose to go for the jugular whilst others choose the subtle and private way out. Meaning they think of the hurt and pain, scandal that their divorce will cause hence they put family, their children first.

NO PARENT ON THE FACE OF THE PLANET CAN BLAME THEIR DIVORCE ON THEIR CHILD AND OR CHILDREN. ABSOLUTELY NONE BECAUSE NO CHILD STOOD UP AND SAID PICK ME. I WILL BE GOOD AND TRUE. I WILL LOVE YOU FOREVER EVER WITHOUT END. WE SHAGGED AND GET YOU, HENCE WE ARE RESPONSIBLE FOR YOU, RESPONSIBLE FOR OUR CHILDREN.

No parent secured their ass or the ass of their child and or children before having them.

TRUST ME SOME PARENTS ARE BITCHES BECAUSE THE ACCEPTABLE NORM NOW IS TO HAVE CHILDREN FOR PROFIT; MONETARY GAIN.

Children have become the acceptable MEDIA OUTLET FOR MANY PARENTS.

To be pregnant is classy but what society does not see is the slew of nannies that are looking after some of these high profile children. As soon as the camera is gone (not filming), the child is handed off and or pawned off to the nanny whilst she goes to the gym or the juice bar including salon for her and or his next fix.

Please!! Mama just using them (their children) for convenience; cameo appearances, her next paycheque, the dollar bill ya'll.

We lack parenthood and parenting skills and wonder why the youths of today turn out the way they do.

We lack morals and wonder why the youths of today are so disrespectful.

We use youths, children as adults and wonder why their lives as so jacked up, messed up and fucked up.

We use children for everything and when they mess up we call them messes and fuck up as well as screw ups. We've forgotten that it is us the adults that fucked them up royally. We the adults are the ones to use our children and turn them into child prostitutes – money hungry slores that are strung out on drugs and alcohol.

We the adults are the ones to allow our children to lay with grown ass men and woman and wonder why some turn out the way that they do. Some are so fucked up that they need psychiatric help – meds to keep them from going crazy. Going fucking insane so that they don't fuck up and off some of us in society.

We the adults are the ones to allow our children to raise children. Babysit and so forth. Babysitting a sibling is okay but when that child becomes the parent then we have a true problem; a serious problem and issue.

We've forgotten that it is us the adult that put these youths and or children in adult clothing and expect them to act like us (adults) as well as become us (adults).

We take their childhood from them but yet say the youths of today are wrong.
Say they are not being raised right and or have no morals.

Think, are we not the ones to give these youths all the tools for failure.

Are we not the ones to tell them to act like us and be like us?

Are we not the ones to raise them wrong?

Are we not the ones to say idolize me, I'm your star, be like me?

Are we not the ones to write books of immorality and say, read these books and try some of the things that are in these books?

Are we not the ones to make videos and movies of immorality and say watch me, this can be you?

Are we not the ones to write laws of immorality and lies and tell the youths, children that these laws are okay when they are not? So how can we truly blame the youths when we as adults fucked them up and jacked them up beyond repair? We as adults have no morals but yet we are expecting our children to have morals.

We as adults are the ones not to care nor do some of us show care when it comes to our children then turn around and expect our children to show us love. You have not true love when it comes to anyone including your children, so why should they show you true love when you have no truth and or true love in you?

We teach them wrong and when they do wrong (as we tell them to do) we chastise them and blame them. How the hell does that work?

We the adults take their future (children's future) from them and expect them to live. How the hell can that be? What good future do these kids (children) have when we've taken all from them? We mess up the planet and rape the planet of its resources then expect our children to clean up our mess – save us from our burdens and or sins. How the hell can we take all in this day and time and expect our children to save us when we've left them with nothing?

We put all on the endangered list without putting self and or humanity on this list. Let's put it this way, our children are on the endangered and or extinct list too because soon they will have nothing; truly have nothing to *save them. We incur debts globally and expect them (our children) to come and bring these debts down. Well what about their debts that they are going to incur? Hence no one thinks of generational sins that continue and or roll over and or accumulate from generation to generation. Nor do we think about the interest and rate of inflation on these debts over time. Hence we as adults and parents including adults and parents of past generations are to blame for the sins handed down to our children because not one of us secured their future and we say we love them; they are our lifelines.*

We as humans have and has put ourselves on the human extinction list with death due to our sins. And instead of getting rid of them; we are waiting for someone to save us. Bail us out of our mess and messes; sins. Think, truly think because he Good God and

Allelujah will never ever without end ordain anyone to come and die for you and your sins. If he Good God and Allelujah did that he would be a murderer like David of your book of sin. He would be a murderer like us humans. Hence he Good God and Allelujah cannot act or go into the way of the wicked; humans.

Can the system change?

Yes if you look at the system as being you.

Like I've said in another book, we are the ones to hand over control of our lives to people that have not our best interest at heart. And when they fuck up our lives we blame the system and or everyone including the devil for our sins and or wrongs and or mistakes.

SIN IS A CHOICE NOT A RIGHT.

DEATH IS A CHOICE NOT A RIGHT AND I'VE TOLD YOU THIS.

Hence when we steal, kill, commit adultery, hate and abuse each other, it's a choice. The choice we made to sin and or do evil therefore giving death life.

Can we learn from the mistake of others?

Yes but how many of us choose to?
How many of us want to learn?

Like I've said in my other books, life is given and we are the ones to live it good, clean and true; positive. We are not to live life negatively but positively.

We can no longer blame others including the devil for our sins because we are the ones to sin not them sin for us.

As youths you have to learn that we cannot continuously choose wrong without consequences. FOR EVERY WRONG WE DO, THERE IS A CONSEQUENCE TO IT. Some may not feel the consequence here on earth but it does not mean they won't feel it in the grave.

As youths you have a choice just like us adults and it's up to you to make the right choices for you. You cannot let someone choose for you because their choice is not your choice. We all have will hence the will to choose either good or evil.

Your choice is not my choice so choose wisely at all times. Yes we do fall but pick yourself up and get back on board because mistakes do happen. I also know that some parents do not care. When things happen at school and my children tell me I ask what about the parents? They would say, mom some parents don't care. So for all of you that have parents that don't care, know that Good God care and so do I. Truly care about you and do good for you. Yes it's hard and you want things to be different well make the difference in your life when it comes to you. Do positive things for you. I know you may need a hug on the days things are not right but think of me hugging you. Think of me telling you everything is going to be okay because it is. Think of me holding you tight and rubbing the nape of your neck or head. There are times when I need a hug and I hug Good God and jump on his back and you can too. You can tell him your jokes. You can hug him and even punch him in the arm as you would a friend. He truly does not mind nor will he sin you for this. So make Good God your father and friend too because he does listen. He does speak because he will tell you when you are wrong. Yes for real you will hear his voice tell you, you are wrong when you are wrong. I would not lie to you because it has and have happened to me. Hence I tell you Good God and Allelujah speaks and do speak for himself when it comes to you or anyone.

Goodness will always be there and we will make it together. Never forget this. Truly listen and start taking baby steps towards helping you. If you are on drugs and want to quit, take baby steps in quitting.

Walk more, meditate, write, listen to music, draw, make a quilt but stay focussed. Will you fall off the wagon from time to time? Yes but pick yourself up and continue on your way. You are not a failure you are strong and growing stronger. Things do happen and the more you overcome these happenings, is the stronger and secure you get in life.

Listen just last week because today is August 31, 2014 and I am editing this book I dreamt this lady. And please do not mind if I toggle between dates because if you've read any of my other books you know I am infamous for toggling between dates. Like I said, I dreamt this lady but I cannot tell you what she looks like because I could not see her. She was singing this song. This is the verse of the song I clearly remember because I got up and wrote it down: *"Although I never made it to the rainbow, I can see your smiling face."* It was as if she was singing to and or for Janelle Monae. I did not see Janelle Monae in the dream but a picture of her with her hair down was embedded in dream for me to remember. This may be weird to you but then my dream world and dream gets weird at times. Some things are hard to explain hence they are vague to you but I do the best I can to explain them the way I know how to. ***So truly do not lose hope because hope is always there. No matter how hard it seems truly do not give up because the*** *_stars as well as the abode of Good God and Allelujah is attainable and reachable. You can get there. All you have to do is try and trust you, trust in you and do more than believe. KNOW._*

Do I fall?

You bet your bottom dollar I do but I pick myself up and go.

There are days that you will feel weak and this is fine. Ly down and think for a few minutes, nap if you have to but after that few minutes, sit up. Now get up and go to the bathroom and wash your face and brush your teeth. Shower and dry yourself off if you have to. Get dressed and have breakfast. If you don't want breakfast, go for a short walk and come back in. Yes there are days when you can't go for a walk and or make it. Then get a good book and read. Draw, sing, write, but do what makes you happy.

Well I am financially stressed out and can't make it. Smile, been there and getting out of it slowly. *_CUT BACK ON YOUR BILLS._* I don't have cable, got rid of it because my children weren't really watching television hence I was throwing away money. Got Netflix instead and the kids are truly loving it because they can watch the programs that they want to watch when they want to watch it. I'm just waiting for Netflix to have more of their own shows. There's this weird British flick called Misfits that they are so into. Orange is the new black they are so into. Me, got to see if they have Doctor Who because I so need to get caught up on this show. Truly love this show but I am years behind in the series. People Netflix is cheap and it's doable so cut back and do what is doable for you and your finances. If you don't need fifty million cell phones don't have them. Find a package that is right for you that give you unlimited text and international text for $5.00 but no more than $5.00 if this is what you need. If a $40.00 package is right for you get the $40.00 package and don't let anyone up sell you. I hate the up selling when it comes to anything. If I want and need you to up sell, I will tell you to up sell me but on my terms not yours. This is what I want and need that can fit my budget do not up sell me. I cannot afford it so don't waste my time and yours. If you up sell, I am going to get annoyed and leave. I know my budget not you. The contracts are locked in. *THE CELL PHONE CONTRACTS ARE FOR THE PHONE NOT THE PLAN.* If you have your phone that works well for you use your phone hence you will not be locked into a contract that you will get dinged for if you have to break your plan. Listen people, I am not a gadget freak hence I truly don't have a cell phone. Maybe I will eventually get one but I highly doubt it. Need my privacy and don't like to talk on the phone twenty four seven. Going for a coffee with a friend where we can talk face to face suits me just fine.

ONWARDS I GO BECAUSE I'VE STRAYED

And yes if that happiness is being completely naked in your house then be completely naked. But if you have kids in the house you cannot be completely naked. Well my husband or wife don't like me to walk naked. Well too bad for them walk naked because some of us our spirit need this, so give this to your spirit even if they are not around. Sometimes your spirit will need organic juice and or a vacation. Give your spirit what it needs providing you can do so. If you can't go on a vacation go on a vacation in your home or backyard. I have to learn to go on a vacation in my home. No, I can't because my vacation is getting away from my children to unwind and destress. And don't you dare go there with the negative things like death and stealing. That is the evil side of your spirit talking and you cannot give the negative side of you what it wants. ***Do good not evil.*** Know that it's harder when your negative side kicks in because negative, your negative side do not want you to prosper hence good and evil will. I'm a mother and I truly like to talk to young kids like you and encourage you. My mother did and I got my education and I know she is proud of me and all of her children. So if you need a mom I am here for you. I may not live with you but I am here to encourage you. Listen to good council and start talking to God – Good God and Allelujah and he will pull you through.

I know some of you need parents, a shoulder to cry on. Well take my shoulder and the shoulder of God – Good God and cry on it.

Your grades are not good and you are struggling. If you have a homework club at school join that club and get the help that you need to help you succeed. Yes you will have friends that will call you a chump if they still use this word. But be the chump because at the end of the day when you are graduating at the top of your class they are not. Every passing grade you get you are at the top of the class. If you are at a 50% strive for a 55% on the next test. Then take it higher until you reach your goal. ___KNOW THAT IN ORDER FOR YOU TO SUCCEED YOU HAVE TO PUT SOMETHING INTO IT. AND THAT SOMETHING IS YOUR TIME AND EFFORT. Don't be like those that say you don't need a education, you do. Hence TRULY DO NOT WASTE YOUR TIME ON EARTH BECAUSE TIME IS PRECIOUS AND IT DOES AFFECT YOUR GOOD FUTURE.___

Take 15 – 20 minutes with your teacher after school to get the help that you need. If the teacher does not have time find someone that is knowledgeable in the course (s) you are having difficulties in and see if he or she can tutor you.

The internet is there. Try and get help with the tutorials they have on line. Truly be careful with these tutorials because some of these tutors do not keep it simple. Even I get frustrated with the internet and finding simple answers. Hence some things are not meant for you to navigate easily with and that's a crying shame.

Your parents are there use them. Meaning let them help you. I do with my children but they don't like when I help them. I get frustrated with them. The simple things you are expecting them to get they don't get it and this is strange to me.

If you know you are a video game freak make sure you get your homework done before you play video games hence avoiding the yelling of your parents. Get what you need to get done before you play video games.

Also, in class ask more questions. Do not stop asking questions until you get the answer you are looking for is simplified. This will help you on your tests as well.

And if music helps you to study and focus listen to music at home whilst studying and or doing homework but not in class. You have to show your teachers respect.

Also, tardiness is an issue with you the younger generation and I have one that is so not tardy when it comes to school. Man waking up is a problem but yet staying up and playing video games isn't. Doing homework and studying is a problem, but yet playing video games and skyping and or face booking and tweeting isn't a problem. Yes the struggle is real for me but I am enduring. But I can only endure for so long before I am gone. The stress is real hence my abundance of gray; gray hair.

As children and young adults you cannot allow anyone to lie to you. I cannot give you relationship advice and or life advice and turn around and divorce my mate and or abandon life. Come on now. Truth isn't about lies, it's about truth, understanding and or over standing; knowledge.

What 's right for this person may not be right for you and what's right for you may not be right for him or her; the next person.

Are there give and takes in life?

Yes, but it all depends on what your give and take is.

I like Jackfruit and you don't. So why would I want to be with you. We are going to have conflict. Hence I stay away from you and find people that truly like and truly love Jackfruit. I am in the group that I truly belong to because what I don't know about Jackfruit they will teach me truthfully and honestly. Hey I truly love Jackfruit and just found out this month August 2014 that you could juice Jackfruit. Mind you I did not like the Del Monte infusion hence I will not buy it. The blend lacked something for me. There are just certain fruits you are not to fuse with others and jackfruit is one of them in my book.

I truly love coconut and pineapple and Del Monte fused the two as well. I like the blend but it did not leave me awe struck. It was nothing to write home about. Give me my coconut water and pineapple juice separate. Don't fuse them.

Listen many parents and adults screwed up your life and now as adults you are screwed up. They took your life away from you and this is sad but it does not mean you are to continue to live screwed up. Break the chain and come new, renew yourself for the better; the better and positive good in life and for life.

I know some of you young men and men have this attitude of she took me to court for child support. Why should I do anything else for my child? And I am telling you to squash and get rid of this thought. Like I've said, your child did not say pick me. You chose her and or him to procreate with. Your child and or children have not right being in your cat and dog fight. This is your child and or children and your right as a parent does not stop at child support. Money is not the basis for truth, true love is. So truly love your child and ensure their life is secure. Do for your child. If you see a dress or a shirt that is $5.00 to $10.00 and you can afford it, pick it up for your son or daughter and give it to them. No you cannot do this all the time but you can do what you can for your child and or children despite your relation with the other parent. You genes and or seed is a part of that child hence he or she is a tree of life as well as a part of your tree of life. Have good trees that will grow up into good trees that will benefit self, family and society (humanity) on a whole. THE TREE OF LIFE THAT THE BOOK OF SIN; YOUR SO CALLED HOLY BIBLE SPEAKS ABOUT IS YOU. We are all the trees of life hence truly secure your good and true life (tree) in life and with life; Good God and Allelujah; you. If he has the children, work something out where you have the children for the summer. On their breaks and or holidays take your child and or children. Make good arrangements with him or her and live by your word of truth. Stop bashing him or her because at the end of the day neither one was faithful. And no I do not bash my exes because my children know the truth. They see it and know it hence God – Good God and Allelujah is good all the time.

Do I cuss dem out? Hell yes I've cussed them out in a couple of my other books. Am I loving it? Yes. Once I cuss you it's done. I've said my peace and I am gone. All is done so leave me the hell alone so we can move on.

Listen when wicked and evil people don't like you they will give you basket to carry water and this has happened to many of you. Hence religion give us baskets with holes to carry water because religion take all from our physical and spiritual life. Our governments give us basket with holes to carry water also because many are indebted to death hence the massive national debts that many have. So because this debt is a national debt, you the individual is a part of this national debt too and you are indebted to death as well.

Many of you are facing prison terms.
Many of you know someone who took the folly road who are dead.

Many of you don't listen no matter how Mama and Daddy talk to you.

Many of you don't have a Mom or Dad but yet you the younger generation is to save us.

How the hell can they (the younger generation and or our children) save us if we mess them up and take away their right and rights to life?

How the hell are they to save us if we destroy all the tools to save them; us?

If we give them (the youths) no skills for success how are they to succeed? And stop with the bullshit of dem fi watch and learn. If you don't teach them to watch the good that you do, how the hell are they going to learn? Not all can watch and learn.

Well mi mada and faada. Stop right there. You are not your mother nor are you your father. And please do not bring genes into this. Your father's life is his life and yours is yours. Yes his sins will follow you but you can change that. You can ask and or tell Good God and Allelujah to protect you and save you from your parent's sin because it's not correct for their sins (your parent's sins) to fall on you. You have your burden to bare and you have your road to travel hence my parent's sins should be theirs. I should not have to pay for their sins. What about my wrongs and or sins that you might incur? *(Yes say this to him (Good God and Allelujah). And yes I know about genes, hence we share our parent's DNA and lineage. And because of this, what sins they don't pay off you as their children have to try and pay off for them).*

It's like baking a cake. You have to know the ingredients that go into the cake. So if you don't tell the child and or youth, you need 1 cup of flour how are they to know?

Memba sey baking powder look like flower hence you are to teach well; good. Come on now.

It's like you telling a youth four quarters equal one, a whole. Now a smartass like me will tell you, you are lying because four quarters does not equal one it equals 4. I see four pieces not one, so how can 4 quarters equal one – a whole. So in many ways we need to stop lying to people especially our youths. Hence truly teach right and not wrong because wrong is confusion. Teach them what they truly need not what they don't need. They don't need wrong so stop forcing and teaching them wrong.

We cannot give them tools for failure and expect them to succeed. They will not succeed they will fail.

Also as parents and friends we need to start listening to the youths of today. Many youths know what they want and go for it. It is up to us as parents and adults to help them along the way positively not negatively.

What you want for them is not what they want for self. Hence many children live out the dream of their parents and truly do not know what it's like to be happy. They become so depressed and despondent that they become bitter. As parents we need to stop this because your dream is not your child's dream. Your child should not live your dream for you. Your dream is your dream and you should have lived it. My mother had a dream for me and that was to be a nurse or doctor. She bought me some of the books I needed for success but Business was my aim and goal. I loved Business hence I took Business in College. Did I become a manager?

No.

But I am marketing my own books with the hopes of taking things further by having my own clothing line for the BIG BOLD AND BEAUTIFUL WOMEN. You know big women are beautiful, all they need is some good and sexy clothing to go with their shape; size.

If your child want to be a doctor or nurse, encourage them to become a doctor or nurse.

Let their future be their choice and not yours. Their happiness is imperative so let them be truly happy. None of us can live in your shadow because your shadow is your shadow. It cannot change hence let your child live and live good. Further, none of us should live in the shadow of God – Good God and Allelujah either because we cannot. He gave us life hence we are to live life good and clean.

We know Good God is there and we are to respect him as well as listen to him. He will never guide you wrong he can only guide you right – true.

Yes your son or daughter may want to walk in your footsteps but let that choice be theirs and not yours.

When good marries evil, that child does not have to turn out good; you will have problems. Hence you have to be constantly praying to Good God and Allelujah for help in raising that child. And if you don't have problems, truly give God – Good God and Allelujah thanks because you are one of the fortunate and blessed ones. You made it.

You've seen the way I've pleaded and begged Good God and Allelujah to help me with mine. It's not an easy road for some of us especially if you are a single parent.

Yes I know it's not easy for some married parents either. But one cannot be pulling this way whilst the other pull in the opposite direction. Both parents must be unified in the decision and or punishment they dish out. And yes if the father and or husband is the stronger one in the punishment department then let him handle it and vise versa.

People, our children are slick. Trust me they know more than me and you. So truly take care and build strong and lasting; truthful relationships with your children and or child. It's wonderful when your child and or children can come to you and tell you of the wrongs they have done. So truly get to know your children. Truly have good and lasting including friendships with them.

You may not have a good relationship with all your children but cherish the good that you have with them because we are all not always going to be there for them. The reality is, some of us will not see our grandchildren grow up so cherish your time on earth with your kids; children. Despite the heartache and pain they give does not mean when you have grandchildren you can't teach them right and do right by them. Grandchildren are precious, hence I will never forget the way my mother was with my first two children before she passed on to a higher and better life to be with Good God and Allelujah. Hence if I get grandchildren I am going to cherish them, take them, spoil them and teach them right and never wrong. Children can be true but how we raise them do make a difference in our lives and theirs. So always choose good over evil because the good you do for your children they will remember and will do all to save you in death. ***However, it does not mean that when they get in trouble you are to constantly bail them out. My children know that if they disobey good and true council and get themselves in trouble they are infinitely and indefinitely on their own. I will not run behind them like some parents and risk it all including go bankrupt for them. Hell to the no.*** *I've counselled you time and time again by talking to you and telling you what I see and you choose to ignore the warnings; then don't come to me looking for help when you are in trouble because I will not help you. I did not fail you as a parent you failed yourself hence I am not going to feel ashamed for your misgivings. Like I've said time and time again, I have one in particular that don't listen. Yes others don't listen. No, two truly don't listen and they are the same sign hence truly woe be unto them when they get older.*

No people, eee cum eeene like tick pap inna dem eease ole. No, I have to wonder if dem ear drum kaake up fi dem nofi listen to reegile. Wow, dem haade ears yu si. Just ask Good God and Allelujah how I bug him and complain to him about them. No, for real people ask Good God and Allelujah. I'm not joking ask him and he will tell you. And for some of you that have read my other books see how I complain and talk about them. Some of you know the heartache and pain I have in raising them because you too feel my pain from what you have read.

Also as kids, our children grow older they are going to want their space and freedom. Give them their space and freedom because they need it. Just as you need space they need their space too and or also.

And yes going out with mom and or dad to the movies they won't want to do after a certain age.

It's August 15, 2014 and I have to interrupt this book because I just had the weirdest dream about my death. So to the Islamic Community I don't give a crap how you try to kill me because of what is said in my other books. I see all before it's done and or your plan take fold.

I don't give a crap how you use children to set me up; try to kill me. THE FACT REMAINS THAT YOU'RE ALL FUCKING MURDERERS AND HELL IS YOUR HOME. HENCE YOU ARE ALL HELL BOUND. YOU TAKE FROM LIFE – THE BREATH OF LIFE HENCE ALLAH; ALLELUJAH HAS NO USE FOR LIARS LIKE YOU. KNOW THIS, BABYLON WILL BE NO MORE SOON BECAUSE THE KING OF DEATH LOST IN 2013 AND I DID SEE A FULL CHARCOAL BLACK MOON.

Not one of you will get into Good God's abode. So no matter how you cry out to Allah, Allelujah WILL NOT HEAR YOU. He does not deal with Babylonian murderers. Babylonians take life and tell lies on him. You say Allah which stands for the Breath of Life but yet you give children weapons to kill –

take a life. You say Allah but yet praise and worship death. You bow down to death because death is your keep and not life. Enmity is in your hearts hence you lie and say God – Good God and Allelujah put enmity between his seed and your seed as written in the Babylonian Book of sin; the dead. Man's so called holy bible as written and translated by Babylonian so – called Jews. Remember this, you prostrate and bow down to death, not I. I know life and the Breath of Life and absolutely no one can bow down to life, they can only live it. Live it good true and clean so that they can GO UP TO GOOD GOD AND ALLELUJAH. HENCE THEIR UPRIGHT EYE IN THE TRIANGLE. ALL THAT IS EVIL MUST GO DOWN AND BOW DOWN TO DEATH; HELL. YOU MUST GO DOWN TO HELL TO DIE HENCE THE DOWNWARD EYE IN THE TRIANGLE THAT WICKED AND EVIL PEOPLE RECEIVE IN THE GRAVE. Your judgement has always been death hence you cannot live good and clean with others. Thus your pledge of death and deceit long before Adam and Eve (Hawwah).

So truly screw the lots of you because HELL IS HOVERING OVER ALL YOUR HEADS LITERALLY.

You tell lies on Allah by saying if you kill you go straight to paradise to see him and that's an infinite and indefinite forever ever fucking lie. The law of GOOD GOD AND ALLELUJAH STATES, "THOU SHALT NOT KILL," and you kill each and every day. YOU TAKE AWAY LIFE FROM ALLAH WHO IS ALLELUJAH AND GIVE IT TO DEATH. SO HOW CAN HE ALLAH AND OR ALLELUJAH TRUST ANY OF YOU WHEN YOU LIVE TO KILL – TAKE ALL LIFE FROM HIM?

How can you say Allah when life (Allah and or Allelujah) knows you not?

How can you say Allah when life (Allah and or Allelujah) is not yours, you are truly not his own but death's own?

You the Islamic community did your jobs and that was to deceive humanity hence the war between

NORTH AND SOUTH CANNOT STOP. You have to kill because your father is DEATH – SATAN. Your father could never be Good God and Allelujah and you the stupid Black People of the West cannot see this. North instigated this hence Nod – the North were locked off from the South long before Adam and Eve; Hawwah in their book of sin – the dead. They the North (Nodites) made sure they incorporated their nasty and polluted history in the books of history; BLACK HISTORY SPECIFICALLY. They polluted our own hence they spread their lies of adultery (polygamy) and incestual history and expect humanity to accept their nastiness of lies and deceit, condemnation and abomination. You're all fucking nasty because you're use to banging your own and pro creating with your own. Hence disease became rampant in your kingdom because you're all whores of the vilest and wickedest kind. Family rams that keep it in the family hence you all have the same whoring last name. You hide your shame by veiling your women because you don't want humanity to know that you are all inbreeders that marry and screw (bang) your own. So truly fuck all of you because DEATH KNOWS YOUR WHORING AND LYING ASSES HENCE THE ENTIRE LOTS OF YOU ARE HELL BOUND LITERALLY. Thus saith the Lord thy God meaning it is so. Hell has and have all of you by your balls because you lie and deceive, seek acceptance when your asses were never accepted by him Good God because you worship other gods and destroy all that is on earth with your condemnation and wickedness; sins. I know your history and trust me it is not clean. It is vile and disgusting hence Good God and Allelujah thought it befitting to separate South from the North. Negative energy from positive energy, hence Psalms One is our keep and reminder of what we must do and how we must live daily forever ever.

You the Islamic Community were what Good God warned his children about. But like disobedient children we did not listen. Hence death came and claimed many of us long before Adam and Eve. Those that became a part of your pathetic garden – the Garden of Eden were your slaves because all they found in that land was brutality, death, murder, heartache and pain, all forms of sin and corruption. Things they did not truly know about until you came along and destroyed them including their precious homes including God – Good God and Allelujah himself. Our disobedience caused him Good God to flee and he's still fleeing because we refuse to listen. We choose not to listen to him hence he's left us to the condemnation and corruption as well as abomination that we've chosen here on earth for self including children. But before doing that he left a part of him in us so that we could call out to him. And that part of him is his name Allelujah. I know for a fact North will not stop fighting against the South because you want what we have and that is true life – Good God and Allelujah; Allah himself. But you truly can't have him because he never belonged to you and never will belong to you. You are the people of fire hence the people and true people of hell. We have the Breath of Life and can get the breath of life at any time. Hence we don't want or need what any of you have. We have life already and trust me I am proud of him as well as proud he's chosen me. I am proud that he (Good God and Allelujah) is a part of my life, so why the hell would I leave him for an imposter; your god and gods. Look at it this way, I have life already, why the hell would I want death to kill me – you? You're all condemned and full of pure sin – evil, hence the negative energy of the North. Trust me you are fighting but you are fighting self because the South must walk away and close its door and doors to all of you. Redemption draws nigh and no matter your money that you accumulate you cannot buy life because LIFE CANNOT BE BOUGHT OR SOLD. All that the devil (Jay Z) will give to you will not save you. So truly keep your resources because it truly cannot get you into Good God and Allelujah's abode. And Good God truly forgive me for the ranting above but these people truly irks me. They use your name like yu an dem a quabs. Dem no noa yu nor do they care anything about you and for you but yet they use your name in their stinking mouths. Yes I know good and evil call upon the Breath of Life but do you truly have to let them use your name in their mouths? Coo pan dem too? Coo pan dem? No Good God, truly coo pan dem.

No, Good God you know the way I am with you. And you know the way I am when I see these death dreams about me. Why the hell should humanity bow down to their gods or any gods for that matter and say it is you when it's not you?

No come on now. We have to do better. They want you and say they are yours but they kill and take life. Tell lies on you and death just sit back an relax like nothing is happening. Cu pan death to. No come on now. Enough is enough with man's religious bullshit of lies and death. You have to do something about this because you are not death, you are life. You can no longer let death impale life. You and I know it's not right nor is it just for Billions to die unfairly and unjustly. No death can be justified, so why are you allowing wicked and evil people to use your name to justify their murderous ways and tendencies? Look at the children Good God and Allelujah. Remember you showed me your children and they were all Jews; Black Jews as well as a Mixture of Black and White. So why are you allowing wicked and evil people to take from their life; your life?

Why are you allowing wicked and evil people to kill them; take away their future and place with you?

I can't stand the thought of losing you so how do you expect a child to? You are our right and hope. Our lifeline and you are allowing people to take that from us and you.

Why?

Can a man or woman create you and all that you have given us?

No right? So why are they taking our right from us – you?

As black people we've forgotten our history hence MARCUS MOSIAH GARVEY SAID, *"A PEOPLE WITHOUT KNOWLEDGE OF THEIR PAST HISTORY, ORIGIN AND CULTURE IS LIKE A TREE WITHOUT ROOTS."* And he's infinitely and indefinitely correct. Islam was our right and roots but when the Babylonians invaded our space and took it over by adding their idol and murderous bullshit to it, he Good God and Allelujah drew the line. He had to make us leave Islam for our own safety. Islam became unclean just like my homeland Jamaica became unclean.

ONCE GOOD GOD AND ALLELUJAH HAS DEEMED SOMETHING, A LAND OR SOMEONE INCLUDING A WAY OF LIVING (LIFE) UNCLEAN AND HE

HAS NOT GIVEN THAT WAY OF LIFE, OR THAT PERSON AND OR SOMEONE AND LAND A SAVING GRACE WE ARE TO STAY AWAY FROM THAT SOMEONE, WAY OF LIFE AND LAND INDEFINITELY FOREVER EVER WITHOUT END. We cannot go back in that fold, thus saith the Lord thy God meaning it is so. But yet we as Blacks and Whites continue to disobey the word and words of God – Good God.

Condemnation is condemnation and Islam is condemned because it leads you to the SLAUGHTER HOUSE OF DEATH; HELL LITERALLY. Your spirit become like pigs because it is unclean. Many of our ancestors accepted the Babylonian Way of Life until this day. We gave up our history and culture to become slaves and or servants (Abdullah) to them; death. Hence our history and culture has and have been diluted to include them. *We the BLACK RACE (NOT BASED ON HUE) ARE THE LAMBS OF BABYLON THAT THEY ARE LEADING TO THE SLAUGHTER HOUSE OF DEATH LITERALLY AND WE CANNOT SEE THIS.*

They feed us a little bit of truth from our own history and we gobble it up like fools. We would rather die like fools when it comes to Islam and religion rather than know the truth and live. <u>Hence many, if not all black lands (lambs) are in disarray.</u> We are poor and wanting whilst others take and rape the land and people of their riches – glory and culture, heritage and home; wealth. We would rather fight alongside the devil and his people rather than walk away from them and accept life. <u>***HENCE I'VE TOLD YOU IN MY OTHER BOOKS HELL IS FULL OF BLACK PEOPLE AND RECRUITING MORE LITERALLY. AND THIS IS BASED ON HUE.***</u> *We keep refusing our calling and it's time to stop it.* As Marcus Mosiah Garvey said, *"Lift up yourselves, men, take yourselves out of the mire and hitch your hopes to the very stars themselves. Let no man pull you down, let no man destroy your ambition, because man is but your companion, your equal; man is your brother; he is not your Lord, he is not your sovereign master."* He also said, *Our UNION MUST KNOW NO CLIME, BOUNDARY, or NATIONALITY...PRACTICE ONE FAITH, that of Confidence in themselves, with ONE GOD! One Aim! One destiny!* <u>***Let no religious scruples, no political mechanism divide us***</u>.*"* Instead of keeping true to our history, culture and god, we gave him up to become slaves, wanting and needing of everything. Our history is being fed back to us in a nasty way and instead of saying no this is not right, you are tainting our history and God, we stand aside and look; praise death and give thanks for the shit that is being fed to us.

TELL A BLACK MAN OR WOMAN ABOUT RELIGION AND HE OR SHE READILY ACCEPTS IT – GOBBLES IT UP. TELL HIM OR HER ABOUT THEIR ROOTS AND CULTURE AND THEY WILL TELL YOU IT ISN'T SO.

To them what they read in the history books is the truth but yet fail to know that their history and culture is engrained in them. Ask them about the civilization of man and or their origins they cannot tell you without quoting books of lies told about them.

We as the BLACK RACE HAS AND HAVE BECOME OUR GREATEST ENEMY AND FOR THIS SATAN TRULY LOVES US. HE CAN PUT HIS POT ON THE STOVE AND KNOW WITHIN A NANA SECOND WE ARE GOING TO SELL OUT OUR OWN GOD AND ACCCEPT THE LIES HE'S TOLD US. AND THIS IS EXACTLY WHAT HE HAS DONE. *(Eve and or Evening and or Hawwah). His lie worked hence the black man has and have rejected his own*

god and accepted the devil's own. Every nasty god on the planet earth is our god; accepted by us and we refuse to realize and know that we are being deceived. Going to go to hell and die. The lie did not work for Eve, Evening and it sure as hell isn't going to work for us in this day and time. She (Eve) died so what say us today? No we are going to die too because JUDGEMENT HAS BEEN ISSUED UPON MAN – HUMANITY LITERALLY. We have been found guilty and it's time to pay up, give death his pay on a massive scale before 2032.

RELIGION IS DECEIT.

RELIGION STEAL ALL FROM US INCLUDING OUR OWN GOD; GOOD GOD AND ALLELUJAH AND WE WONDER WHY THE BLACK RACE IS SO FUCKED UP, JACKED UP AND MESSED UP.

We left our own for shit and wonder why he Good God does not communicate with us as well as bother with us.

Why the hell should he when he knows as soon as im tun im back wi sell im out and praise other gods. We forgot the "THOU SHALT NOT HAVE OTHER GODS BEFORE ME LAW" hence NOT ONE OF US IS LOYAL TO HIM GOOD GOD AND ALLELUJAH AND THAT IS A CRYING SHAME.

We are sell outs that would rather walla inna dung (shit) an cry bout things hard, and how life nuh fair. Well if we had listened to him in the first place and stayed loyal to him instead of giving him up; shit that is happening to us would not be happening.

We want what the next man has hence we've become covetous backbiters that seek the hurt and downfall of our own including Good God and Allelujah and that's a shame.

Many of us have and has become educated fools. Sorry slaves that would rather keep us down instead of elevating self, the black community and our children with the true truth of our roots and culture including hair.

WE'VE BECOME VALUELESS BECAUSE WE SELL IMMORALITY AND GIVE UP GOOD FAMILY VALUES.

*No wonder we are the way we are. Always wanting and waiting on God – Good God and Allelujah to come and rescue our lazy asses. We sit there and wait for him Good God to bring us a little bickle – food. Get off your ass and do for you. He Good God and Allelujah is no one's servant – slave. Nor will he swoop down and or rain down insects (locust of nastiness) for you to eat. **If you are not trying to help yourself how the hell can he truly help you?**

How the hell are you going to get help? *We've become nasty hence we've made Good God and Allelujah out to be nasty like us.* Look at us. We believe in this lie. *We believe Good God would give us unclean and unhealthy food like bugs – locust to eat. Good God and Allelujah is not nasty, man – humans are the ones that are nasty because we eat all kind of filth (shit) and say it is good food.* Come on now.

GOOD GOD IS CLEAN AND HEALTHY PEOPLE, NOT NASTY AND UNCLEAN LIKE US.

Stop making him out to be unclean because he's not dirty like us like I've said. We are the nasty ones and expect him Good God and Allelujah to come along with us on our nasty journey and or pathway; ride. Get a clue and life. He Good God will not follow you because he follows no one. We are the ones to follow him meaning live by our cleanliness and truths. Come on now.

We are to praise him by giving him thanks and even this we can't even truly do.

I will repeat. The message on the school wall said, *"FOR GOD SO LOVE US, HE IS WORTHY TO BE PRAISED."* And like I've said, I have a problem with this message because HE GOOD GOD AND ALLELUJAH

SHOULD NOT HAVE TO TELL US HE'S WORTHY TO BE PRAISED. WE ARE TO KNOW THIS AND PRAISE HIM; THANK HIM FOR ALL THE GOODNESS HE'S DONE FOR US. We are to thank him for our bads; downs because some of us learn from the wrongs we have done and we also teach our children not to do these wrongs.

If you don't get off your ass how the hell are you going to get food and or help? Help isn't going to come to you like that, so truly do the good that you can to help you and for you. Life isn't a game, it's real and if you don't want it then the devil will surely take it.

Yes sometimes we feel bad as if we can't make it but God is there. Tell him how you feel and let him show you what to do to heal you. He gave me Aloe and pineapple in water and it's me that have not exercised the uses of this medicine. Trust me I have to if I am to heal my body. So trust him to help you and heal you.

Onwards I go. IF YOU KNOW NOT YOUR ROOTS AND CULTURE, HOW THE HELL DO YOU EXPECT TO KNOW WHERE YOU ARE COMING FROM AND WHERE YOU'RE GOING?

<u>SHIT YOU CAN'T GO NOWHERE IF YOU DON'T KNOW WHERE YOU ARE COMING</u>

<u>**FROM OR WHERE TO PUT IT.** *Meaning if you know not your address and home you left, how the hell can you go back to it?*</u>

As blacks we truly don't think because all we believe is that we are children of slaves. I'm not. Many of you are but I am not nor do I class myself as one. No one can come and tell me I am a descendant of slaves because Slaves did not make and create this universe, Good God and Allelujah did and he's not a slave. Man turned other human beings into slaves not God. We the black race as in banner not colour of skin created it all with Good God and Allelujah, hence I know life, the truth of life – HIM.

As he Marcus Mosiah Garvey said, "Having had the wrong kind of education, the Negro has become his own greatest enemy." And he is so correct. Instead of knowing the truth of self, our own true history and culture; we would rather let others teach us garbage of self and say this is who we are when we are not.

We would rather let others categorize us and break us up in colours whilst classing us lower than animals and this is wrong. Yes I know we are not all Good God's people but we are his children and he does care. We cannot continue to accept everyone's way and say we belong because we truly do not belong. The Babylonian Way is their way and not ours but yet we fail to see this.

We the Black Race (not based on hue) have a history of our own and we are to know it and cherish it. There are two banners in life, one black and one white. Many blacks fall under the white banner hence I tell you to know yourself – the sins that you do. We created death when we began to sin hence there is a life and death instead of a life only.

We know evil exist but instead of teaching right we teach wrong and follow sin to our deaths whilst taking our children with us.

WE CAN NO LONGER SACRIFICE OUR CHILDREN TO DEATH. COME ON NOW.

WE HAVE TO TAKE CARE OF THEM AND GIVE THEM A CHANCE TO LIVE. When we take it all from our children, what future do they have?

Hell is real and it's not fair to send our child (ren) to hell to die, come on now. Think because the life you save is your own.

ONWARDS I GO BECAUSE I'VE STRAYED.

They (the Babylonians) tainted Islam hence ISLAM IS NOT CLEAN. WE ALLOWED DIRTY AND NASTY PEOPLE INTO OUR HOME HENCE ISLAM WAS CONDEMNED. Not one of us was to walk in the way of Islam again because it is polluted and will forever be polluted because of the Babylonians. They teach death, teach their children to kill, live promiscuously by having more than one wife hence their adulterous and incestual ways.

- ❖ *They break every law of cleanliness.*
- ❖ *They break every law that he Good God and Allelujah has and have given to us.*

- ❖ *They are liars just like their father Satan. He lied to Eve (Evening) told her she would not die. Told her she would become a God.*

She did not become a God, she died and lost her place with him Good God and Allelujah and still humanity cannot see this.

The lie did not work for Eve and now you are told Jesus is going to save you when you of yourself sinned to go to hell. He Good God and Allelujah does not deal in death. He gave us good and true life and we abandoned that life. We gave our life up and accepted death. Hence billions accept Jesus and Jesus never existed. Jesus represents death. He was the son of the mother of death (Mary) in your so called holy book – the bible. Man no matter how you change the story it will always read the same. *Go back to your Nimrod and Semiramus all the way back to father and daughter, Adam and Eve.*

Jesus represents death because death existed in Babylon (the North). It never existed in the South but when Hawwah (Eve and or Evening) united with death (Sin and or Satan) due to the lie, sin was born in the South. Please do not associate this with the Garden of Eden because Sin's Garden is not Good God's Garden nor is Sin's Garden clean. Death was in Adam's Garden hence he sinned by procreating with his own daughter. (Incest). Yes you are confused but let it stay this way because the story of Genesis is written in layers for humanity not to comprehend and or over stand. Meaning if you do not know the different layers and or doors of the bible you cannot open them and or this book.

Death cannot save anyone death can only kill you physically and spiritually. We all know this but yet are deceived into thinking death hath life when death hath none.

I refuse to fall in death's trap. So with all the traps you the Islamic Community set for me truly good luck because HELL IS WAITING FOR ALL OF YOU LITERALLY. Hell has always been your home but humanity has and have forgotten this.

AND TO THE BLACK SELL OUTS THAT GO AGAINST HIM GOOD GOD AND ALLELUJAH. TRULY WOE BE UNTO TO YOU BECAUSE IF YOU THINK YOU KNOW HELL, TRULY WAIT UNTIL TOMORROW WHEN YOU GET THERE. And truly know the time frame of tomorrow because tomorrow could be three months and or six months from now. It could also be one year from now or a thousand years from now.

You gave up Good God and Allelujah for a place in hell literally because HELL IS FULL OF BLACK PEOPLE AND LITERALLY RECRUITING MORE. (Islam and Christianity – all facets of religion). I know what hell looks like because I've seen it. I've seen the graves and headstones of all of you; hence I know what the Islamic Community will do to get you to follow them straight to hell.

The plan worked because RELIGION IS THE FOUNDATION AND BASIS OF MAN – WICKED AND EVIL PEOPLE. HENCE YOU FOLLOW THE RELIGIONS OF THE WICKED. WICKED AND EVIL PEOPLE – MEN.

If he Good God and Allelujah tell you:

❖ *THOU SHALT NOT KILL*

❖ *THOU SHALT NOT COMMIT ADULTERY*

❖ *THOU SHALT NOT HAVE OTHER GODS BEFORE ME*

❖ *THOU SHALT NOT COVET YOUR NEIGHBOURS WIFE*

❖ *THOU SHALT LOVE YOUR NEIGHBOUR AS YOU LOVE THYSELF*

❖ *THOU SHALT NOT STEAL amongst others. We do not listen then what say you? Are we not the disobedient child and or children? So if we disobey him, why should he save us or even listen to us and or our prayers; words?*

All this and more we were told not to do and we do it anyway. We should be listening to him and not listening to others teach us wrong and tell us to do wrong. The pain in the physical is great but the pain and suffering in hell is greater. Ah man I can see the demons of hell smiling right now and rubbing their hands because they know their payday shortly. Trust me they are patiently awaiting that time when all hell will break loose and let loose on your spirit.

So why are we listening to others tell you lies WHEN YOU AND I KNOW DISOBEDIENCE IS A SIN? A first class and one way ticket to hell.

When we disobey him Good God and Allelujah we go directly to hell and die.

When we break the law and laws of him Good God and Allelujah, we are saying to him, watchya man, Gad, Good God yu si mi, mi nuh respek yu, mi nuh rate yu, mi respek an rate death ova yu because a death ova life mi sey.

A death mi a pree because a death mi si, a nuh yu mi si.

Death a mi Gad an yu, yu plug out an log out because death stronga and great dan yu. Das why mi tell di people and my people to pree death and accept death over life. Live fi death. A same thing di church dem du and sey. An dem sey dem cum from yu. So if dem cum from yu and sey a dis wi fi du, wha mek wi caane du it? Nuh yu sey suh? So how cum yu a change yu mine all of a sudden?

Yu caane tell wi fi du something den tun roune an sey it wrong. Yu nuh sey yu a Gad, so how can God be wrong? Death over life mi a pree. And yes this is some of our attitudes today. We justify wrongs when we know beyond a shadow of a doubt that they are wrong. If you know something is wrong, do not accept it and if you do accept it, know and learn when to walk away in truth.

This is the reality of us people. We accept death because our ministers and or clergy tell us to accept death over life.

Our parents tell us to accept death over life.

Our friends tell us to accept death over life. And don't say no, they don't. I am telling you they do. From your friend tell you to do something wrong like disobeying your parents they are telling you to accept death and the punishment of death; hell. If your parents say Joseph do not go to the mall and hang out today, then don't go. Obey them because you don't know what might happen. Someone in your group could steal something and you get caught up in the melee.

You could go and a stray bullet reach you.

You could go and a fight ensue. So truly learn to listen to your parents. And yes I know not all parents are good because some of them teach you to steal and do things you are not to do. Hence TRUST ME

WHEN I TELL YOU, HELL IS TRULY WAITING ON THEIR ASS. Youth man, the sun is hot, but hell is infinitely and indefinitely hotter than that of our sun. Hence the fire (sun) that heats up earth is not the fire that kills the spirit. This is a special type of fire that is designed for this – our sins. So truly know what you are doing. Yes you can correct your parents if they tell you to do wrong. But it's not all parents that will listen and take heed.

Not all parents have good relationships with their children and this is sad.

Right now we are too late because I've been dreaming more and more about youths; the younger generation and it is sad that we as parents have and has screwed you the younger generation up and over.

It's sad that we are the ones to fuck up your lives so that you do not have a future and or anything to look forward to.

AS HUMANS AND PARENTS WE'VE FORGOTTEN THE TRUE LOVE THAT HE GOOD GOD AND ALLELUJAH HAVE AND HAS FOR US. His choice are CHILDREN but yet we do not do right and good by our children.

❖ *We allow others to mess them up.*

- ❖ *Molest them*
- ❖ *Abuse them*
- ❖ *Steal their lives from them*
- ❖ *Rape them*
- ❖ *Kill them*
- ❖ *Send them to hell and die*

Now tell me this, how can he Good God and Allelujah save us when we do all to hurt self, others, our children and Good God himself? We do all that is evil to our children and others and say we love them. We don't truly love them, we hate them. Hate them to the point of killing them. And don't you dare throw this book and say I am a fucking liar. And don't you dare yell at me either and tell me you love your child and or children because you truly don't. And down with the death threats and nasty emails too. I don't have your email you are saying. You will have it and or get it at the end of this book.

Listen when you baptize and christen your child and or children, you've accepted death for them. You gave them – your child and or children over to death, hence making them your sacrifice unto death. There is no father son and holy ghost. The father, son and holy ghost is death, your 666 and even this analogy is wrong because death is time in time, a point in time at that moment in time. Hence the cycle of death is every 6 thousand years. Meaning each generation and or race is given a chance to accept truth. And if you do not accept truth within that cycle of time, then you have to wait another 6 thousand years before the cycle comes around again. During this time more wars come, more killings and diseases come. Let's put it this way, more brutality comes within the new cycle before your eventual death. Hence the mountain that each messenger of God must climb to receive his and her message so that they can save Good God's people. Therefore mountains are significant to truth – life. So when you baptize and christen your child and or children you are handing them over to death as a sacrifice as I've said. Hence telling death he or she can take your child at any time. And yes this is also why some children die before their time. And it matters not if the child dies of a disease or catch a disease and or die of crib death.

Death's arsenal is not limited to weapons – guns. Diseases are a part of death's arsenal because it's death's children – people that create and manufacture these sinful things.

It's death's children – people that give you genetically modified foods laced with herbicides and pesticides for you to eat and kill yourself by. Hence the white race is the sick race because they do sick and evil things.

And please do not base this on hue, colour of skin. This is based on spiritual wickedness – evil and or sins; CURSE. The hue of skin – flesh serves as a reminder of the two deaths. Physical and Spiritual death hence the Ying and Yang, the Blue and White Nile. And for those of a higher learning that have been waiting for confirmation should know that WHITE CANNOT CHANGE. WHITE IS XX AND BLACK AND OR BLUE IS XY. Hence white remains the same in both worlds; the physical and spiritual.

WHITE IS NEGATIVE ENERGY HENCE TRUE DEATH COMES IN WHITE AND IS WHITE IN HUE AND COLOUR OF CLOTHING IN THE SPIRITUAL REALM. *This is the best way I can explain it without confusing you. And I will repeat, when evil dies in the spiritual realm, evil dies as white person; dressed in white and it matters not if you are black. The evil spirit inside of you is white in hue; person and cannot change.*

Physical death is truly not death but we say death because the flesh hath no life because the spirit is gone. The flesh must go back to the ground for the wombs to eat it. Hence in a way the body replenishes the soil. I know this is not the best way to put it but I am going to leave things at this because this is the only way I know how to explain things.

How can he Good God and Allelujah save us when we put guns and ammunition in the hands of little boys and girls and tell them to kill – take a life?

Yes I know everyone is saying well I can't see God and look how long we've been hearing about the coming of Christ and can't see him? Well God is not Christ and he Good God and Allelujah cannot come into a dirty planet. We polluted the planet and when we did this, we were and still telling him Good God and Allelujah we don't want him here with us on earth.

Now I ask you this, how many of us can see death when the spirit has and have left the flesh?

Not many, hence how can he Good God send you a spook and or spirit when you of yourself is human – alive and in the flesh?

Good God and Allelujah cannot send you anyone that is not of him to save you. He has sent you his messengers but because of hate many of you refuse them. THEY WERE NOT THE RIGHT COLOUR AND THEY DID NOT PREACH AND TEACH EVIL TO ACCOMMODATE YOUR LYING AND THIEVING BELIEFS; WAYS.

THE TRUTH IS NOT WITH MAN HENCE HE GOOD GOD AND ALLELUJAH HAS AND HAVE TRULY LEFT US – LET US GO. We continuously refuse to listen to the truth. So how can he Good God and Allelujah save us if we refuse to listen to him? Like I said, we are disobedient children that do not listen to good and true council. We would rather listen to false teachings and beliefs as well as teach our children in the like manner of these false teachings and beliefs rather than save self – our children.

We cannot listen nor can we hear but yet we are expecting our children to. How the hell does that work? If we don't listen how can our children listen? If we don't listen, how can they tell you what's wrong with them?

If we set bad examples for our children are they not going to come and follow those bad examples?

Good God and Allelujah is not a man; he is male and female – pure energy. And I am not expecting any of you to comprehend this because you do not truly know him.

We say him in reference to his spiritual nature and attributes and her in reference to his physical nature and attributes. Hence he Good God and Allelujah is hard to explain to those who truly do not know him. And please do not put colour to him because in truth he Good God is not human or flesh, he is pure energy like I've said. He will however show you him as a person because that's all you know. But never ever draw him as a human. This is severely as well as infinitely and indefinitely wrong. I repeat; do not draw Good God and Allelujah as a human because he is truly not a human. His banner is black but it does not mean he's a black man or a white man. Hence you were told not to make graven images of him or have other gods before him.

As humans we would rather accept lies and die rather than accept the truth. And it is only when WE GET DOWN TO THE CRITICAL HOUR AND OR NANA SECOND, WE RUN TO HIM FOR A SAVING GRACE.

When the plane is almost leaving we are running with baggage in hand to try and catch it. Honey it's too late because the doors are closed and the plane left long ago. THE PLANE YOU ARE NOW RUNNING FOR IS THE PLANE OF DEATH. And this is what's happened to humanity right now. Good God's plane left and we are the ones running to catch it. Why let it go in the first place? He's given us all that is good and true and we are the ones to let it go for what? Death can't save me. Death can only kill me and you so why not live for life all the days of your life and let life truly save you? Teach your children about life and the goodness of life so that they can have life and live. If you have life, teach your children about life so that they can live like you if not better than you. *TRUTH IS EVERLASTING LIFE BUT LIES ARE DEATH; DEATH OF FLESH AND SPIRIT.*

Listen, I've told you about my homeland being unclean time and time again. I cannot go back there (to my homeland) until the land becomes clean again. So do not let him Good God and Allelujah deem you unclean because if he does, you are truly doomed. What is unclean to Good God is truly that nasty and filthy. It means all the stench and garbage piled up globally in our landfills combined is cleaner than that person and or land. It means our sins are so filthy that you cannot imagine what it looks like in reality.

When he Good God and Allelujah say this land or person is unclean we have to stay out of these lands infinitely and indefinitely or until that land and or person becomes clean again.

To disobey God – Good God and Allelujah is automatic death. Meaning when the spirit leaves the body – flesh, you go directly to hell and there is no saving grace issued to you and I've told you this already. Trust me, you will feel it here on earth too because you and your country will begin to lose it all. You called up evil on yourself hence the demons of hell can do anything they want with you. And worse yet if you have a child and or children because at a certain age, the demons of hell begin to play havoc on their senses. They nudge your children and or child to do bad things. And I am speaking from experience. Demons know the dark hence they use the darkness to come to your child. Some do not show their faces hence some are faceless in the dark. So when the church speak of demons they don't know what the hell they are talking about because their definition and perception of demons is child's play compared to the real thing. Hence some of your bad ass children are locked in hell by these demons. Their cross is inverted people hence there is absolutely no saving them. Death and or murder is a must for them. They have to kill and kill until they are caught and or die. If your child or anyone has an inverted cross, they are telling you they are a true demon of hell hence they are bound by the cross. As in the cross you see atop the whore houses of death (churches). Hence the cross is known as the cross of death. So when you go to church you go to the house of death to pay death and pay homage to death.

If he Jesus say he can save you in the grave of your direct disobedience THEN TRULY GOOD LUCK TO HIM BECAUSE HE IS TRULY GOING AGAINST GOOD GOD AND ALLELUJAH. TRUST ME HE TOO IS GOING TO BURN LIKE A BITCH IN HELL JUST LIKE YOU. ABSOLUTELY NO ONE CAN GO AGAINST THE DIRECT ORDERS OF GOD – GOOD GOD AND ALLELUJAH. IF YOU DO, YOU ARE GOING TO DIE. YOU ARE GOING TO FEEL EVERY PUNISHMENT OF DEATH – THE DEMONS OF HELL IN THE LIVING AND IN DEATH; THE GRAVE. HENCE WE ARE TO "HONOUR THY (OUR) FATHER AND THY (OUR) MOTHER THAT THY DAYS BE LONG," AND THAT MOTHER AND

FATHER IS GOOD GOD AND ALLELUJAH HIMSELF. We are to listen to his good and true words as well as know his words and him. We are to keep his good word because they are life – our saving as well as life's grace. If we do not form a good and true relationship – bond with him how can we hear him or even know him when he speaks? Thus we are to have a good and true relationship with him so that we can listen, hear and obey him so that when death comes we are saved. Meaning death pass over us and pass us by. He will never steer us wrong but yet we listen to others tell us otherwise; even tell us lies about him and on him. If he Good God gave us life and truth, why do we say otherwise?

If he Good God is giving us all that is positive, good and easy, why are we saying no, we want things the hard way? What sense does that make? Listen, if I am getting things the easy, good and positive way with him Good God and Allelujah without stress and heartache, hell yes I am going to keep this way infinitely and indefinitely as well as teach you and my children; family so that you can share in the positivity. Why the hell would I want to see you suffer when I myself know the hardships and pain that comes with sufferation. Trust me when you come to my door giving me your god, it's like get lost I have my God already and I truly do not need yours. Why the hell should I give him up for yours and I am more than happy and contended with him. I know the protection and truth I have with him. He does not look down on me because I am not financially well off but yet in all that I have, I am more than financially well off and blessed because my wealth is not determined by the amount of money I have in our bank account. My goodness and truth is my wealth and as long as I am generous in truth and goodness; positivity then I am good to go.

Some of us, including children need to clear the clutter in our homes and closet; lives and we will see just how wealthy we are. Trust me we don't need clutter hence you have people that clean their homes every spring and summer. My son cleaned out the clutter in my living room people and my house feel so light and blessed. Hence I have to do more cleaning as well as organization when it comes to my books and junk mail. To be honest with you, we don't need a lot to live. It is better to save and live on little rather than have it all and waste it all. Many things I am finding that I truly don't need and I have to get rid of the things I truly don't need.

Clutter is messy hence we have to unclutter self and home. I cannot live for extinction like everyone else. Humanity live for extinction because we continuously sin daily and I cannot do that because "the wages (pay) of sin is death. I truly love me and truly love my life despite the hardships to just han it ova to death suh. Come on now. It's a foolish and wicked man and or person that truly do not love self that would hand over his or her life to death. What can death offer me apart from death? So why sacrifice self and children to death if you know you are going to die? Come on now.

We say life then do all for life not death.

If we don't live for life how do we expect to live?

When you are a trying person things do not come easy. You have to persevere and sometimes you do give up. On the days you give up. Regroup and come fresh and go at it again and I've told you this already. *Listen, I am out there handing out flyers for my books and I never knew just how hard it is. When I hear people saying how hard it is trying to make it in the business I can truly stand up and say I know. The pathway to success is not easy nor is it short, it is long. A long and painful journey because you have to contend with so many different spirits and trust me I've seen it in my own black community. The help you seek sometimes in not there. Trust me you are fed lines and if you believe some of these lines, then you are sadly mistaken because they are lies. But with all that said, do not give up do you hear me. Truly do not give up because people will not make it easy for you and they don't especially those in the black community. Too much damn crab inna barrel. Suh wey mi du, mi carve out a likkle ole fimi self and come out. I am doing to help me in the manner that I see befitting. Hence I am infinitely and indefinitely not relying on anyone in the black community for help. I am relying on me and Good God himself. I know what I want and need hence I am doing what I want need to help me. It may take years to get where I need to go but those years are my trying, me trying to get there on my own and not on the backs of others or the help of others.*

So youth man, don't give up if you are trying. Better must come one day. Today may not be for you but tomorrow is yours. So do all the good and positive things you can to get your tomorrow. When you get your tomorrow watch out for the vulture's dem. Make sure you save to ensure when you fade, you have something to fall back on. Remember, no one knew you when you were starving and trying like me. Now that you make it dem a go run cum. But bun dem and run dem. BUT BUILD THOSE THAT TRULY HELPED YOU. Along the way you will meet genuine and nice people and those genuine and nice people you are to give thanks to. Raise them up if you can, but if you cannot, a true and simple thank you will do. Never forget your community because if you get to the status where you can help your community, truly help your community. It matters not if that help is exercise books, pens and pencils including erasers for your community school do it. If you get a chance to go back and talk to the youths, go back and talk to them. Encourage them because you were there and you left out, got out. Show them how to elevate themselves by putting down the guns and focusing on school. Some will not listen, but the ones that truly want better for self will listen and they too will get out. Guns and ammunitions are not positive. They are tools to kill self and others; negative. We cannot create a life and or get back that life we have taken so why take it? Why allow someone to give you a gun to hurt and or kill someone. When you do that you mess up your life, your family's life as well as your community's life. Look at it this way. Your community is deemed bad; gun town. No one wants to live there and many people avoid your community like the plague. Labels are now given to your community, funding becomes scarce; some people don't look at your resume when they read and see your address. Schools are run down and stereotyped. All that is negative is associated with your community, so why do what you do? You can't blame the system you have to blame you. Some communities become hang out for gangs. So basically you are not helping but contributing to the problem. You are the root of the problem. *Tell me something, is it necessary to be gang affiliated?* I know many of you are recruited in a violent and vicious way *and now I am talking to you the gang leaders of the world. Is it worth it and or necessary for you to take a life, bully people and send them to hell with you? You made a choice to ride or die. You made a choice to kill yourself and go to hell and die a more brutal death. So why take others especially children with you? Let me tell you this. All that you do on earth try taking it to hell with you and see how far you get? Try bullying death and the demons of hell. Go on try because I know they are rolling on their bellies with foot up in the air pointing and laughing at the lots of you. Your time is up and your name and number; allotted time in hell is written on your containment unit in hell. So what say you on earth when death comes to collect his pay from you?*

Now look up and view the sun.

See it?

Okay now cry because that sun isn't going to burn you. Yes it's hot but the heat and or fire that is going to burn you in hell is infinitely and indefinitely hotter.

Now see that boiling water on the stove. When you cry out for a little water to cool your spirit and quench your thirst. You are going to get hotter than that boiling water to drink in hell to quench your thirst.

But that's not cooling me, that's killing me you are saying.

Look up again and read the sign that says, "WELCOME TO HELL."

You badass children had better start crying now because you are no exception to the rule. You do not listen to good council and you do all that is bad, so this (hell) is going to be your domain as well.

If you have done bad things to your parents and grandparents including family members and friends, seek their forgiveness if they are still alive. Once they have forgiven you in the living then your slate is wiped clean because that person forgave you. Life isn't about hurt and it's not hurt for hurt because there is a hell. It's just us as humans that have forgotten about it (hell).

As a society we do not think for self. We let others think for us and this is sad. We talk about ghettos and I am going to say this again. **_THE GOVERNMENT DID CREATE GHETTOS WE THE PEOPLE DID._**

The little that the government give us we are the ones to turn the area into slums, gun town, crack houses, whores houses, you name it we did it.

We are the ones to allow undesirables that do not live in our community to come in and mash it up and den wi complain how di area bad. **_IF YOU DO NOT LET THE DEVIL INTO YOUR COMMUNITY, COUNTRY AND OR HOME THE DEVIL CANNOT COME IN._** Come on now. *There is no way in hell can he come in if you refuse him and or don't let him in. So when I hear politicians talk about making the government accountable and or some say they will be accountable if they are elected into office. What the hell are you going to be accountable for?*

I sure as hell know when gang warfare and or violence break out you are going to run and hide, sit your ass down and not stand up and say you are accountable for what has happened.

So politician be clear and specific. *In all your teachings, if you are teaching good and people are not listening then you cannot be accountable for the wrongs that they do. Nor can you say, you need more funding from the government to go into this, this and this. I do not agree with that. <u>If the government laid and get my child then yes I will hold the government accountable for neglect but none of us can.</u>*

*As parents like I've told a councillor that is running for office, as parents we are to be held accountable for our children. We had them hence we are to teach them right. I will not blame the government and put a strangle hold and or noose around the governments neck for our neglect. Find some of these damned deadbeat fathers and mothers and let them be accountable for their damned children. <u>**They had them so why the hell should everyone else in society pay for their damned neglect?**</u> There are no neglect lines when it comes to Good God and Allelujah, so why the hell should there be one with humanity.* If you know you do not want children then don't bleeping have them? Why the hell should I work so damned hard to ensure my children get something when I am dead and the government take it from me and give it to you? Why the hell should I be working for your lazy ass? Come on now. Some people abuse the system hence funding was cut. Yes it's disheartening but this is the reality of life. *WE ARE ALL LOOKING FOR SOMEONE TO BLAME INSTEAD OF BLAMING SELF. We are the ones* *looking for someone to carry the cross for us when we of ourselves can carry it on our own. Meaning we refuse to put down sin and elevate self.*

We want to work but don't pay taxes but this cannot be. How is the country going to run and pay its employees? Yes government waste and this we as taxpaying citizens should hold our governments accountable for. Why the hell are you wasting my tax dollars?

<u>Why the hell are you using my tax dollars to go fight another man's war? Bleep them and let them solve their own damned problem. You put yourself in your mess, get yourself out of it. I am not going to fight your war and disobey God. My people and land is precious. Nor am I going to take your damned refugees. You displaced them you take care of them. And if I take any in good faith, I am going to send you a bill every month for medicine, shelter, food, taxi and bus fare, plane fare to bring them back to your country, plus I am going to charge you for clothing and if they go to church, I am going to tax you for religion because religion is taxable to your God not mine.</u>

We want the easy way in life but yet forget that you have to put your time and effort into things for it to become easy. Yes it was easy long ago, but we are the ones to give up life for death, hence all that is stressful and hard comes. We take away from our lives and this is sad. And truly don't say no you don't because STRESS take away from your life.

* ❖ **The unnecessary yelling you do take away from your life.**

* ❖ **The over eating and drinking that you – we do, take away from our life.**

* ❖ **The unsafe sex you practice take away from your life and the person you are fornicating with. (Adultery times 2)**

* ❖ **The sins we do infinitely and indefinitely take away from our lives physically and spiritually.**

* ❖ **The diseases humans create and design take away from our lives.**

* ❖ **The diseases that we give sexually to others take away from our life and their life. (Aids, Gonorrhea, Herpes, Syphilis)**

❖ *The nagging you do of your husband and or wife including children take away from our lives.*

❖ *The one sided relationships some of us have take away from our lives.*

Yes there are many more but I truly do not want or need this book to be that long.

ONWARDS I GO BECAUSE I'VE STRAYED AGAIN

Humanity live for extinction. *We live to become sacrifices to death hence we are sins sacrifices unto his god who is death.* And I've told you this in another book.

We are the ones that refuse to save self because JUST LIVE EVE WAS FOOLED, WE ARE BEING FOOLED TODAY BY RELIGION AND RELIGIOUS BELIEFS; Religious bullshit, stench – filth and fecal matter.

Like I said, no one should tell you to break the laws of Good God and Allelujah nor should anyone tell you to die. Satan basically called Good God and Allelujah a liar and Eve (Evening) believed him. She trusted Satan (Death) over life and lost. She died spiritually and physically and she is going to die spiritually real soon. When you break the laws of God – Good God you are sinning hence being disobedient. Disobedience of God – Good God and Allelujah is automatic death of spirit.

Know this. **WHEN YOU FOLLOW RELIGION AND ITS BELIEFS YOU ARE BASICALLY CALLING GOOD GOD AND ALLELUJAH A LIAR JUST LIKE SATAN DID.** He, Good God and Allelujah gave us life and when we give it up for death we are basically spitting in his face and saying, you are a damned liar. I am still living and I am enjoying all the goodness of life death has to offer because I worship death and bow down to death. And none of us can say this is a lie because virtually all in humanity believe in death, the Jesus lie. We say we have to die to get to heaven and or paradise whichever one you choose and I've told you, no one can die to see God. You must live good and true; clean. You have to live a positive and clean life whilst trying your best to separate and stay away from all facets of evil. Yes it's hard in the beginning but it gets better over time.

Good people do not have to worry about death in time. Evil people must worry about death in time because they are the ones that were given time in time to amend their dirty and unclean ways.

But I am going to lose my flesh and I don't want to. I want to live. Some will lose their flesh because of sin and the sins that surround us. But eventually this will stop; cease indefinitely. Like I've told you, we were not to lose our flesh, body and spirit was ordained to go directly to Good God and Allelujah but because of sin and the acceptance of death, the two must be separated and this is unfortunate. And yes for those who truly do not know. This is why the spirit has hue, the hue of your physical being.

IF THESE PEOPLE THAT SAY THEY CARED TRULY CARED, THEY WOULD NOT TELL YOU TO SIN AND OR DISOBEY THE LAW AND LAWS OF GOOD GOD AND ALLELUJAH. NONE WOULD, NOT EVEN OUR GOVERNMENTS. But because we don't respect Good God and Allelujah nor do we care about him, we break his law and laws anyway; daily.

We pretend like he does not exist hence we do not have good and true values when it comes to him and life.

We disrespect his law and laws and do what we feel like doing AND FORGET THAT DEATH IS TIME, A TIME IN TIME. THE MORE WE BREAK HIS LAW AND LAWS IS THE MORE DEATH COMES. The longer and further our spirit go into hell to die.

YOU CANNOT SEE THIS, SEE DEATH, BUT I CAN HENCE I'VE TOLD YOU IN COUNTLESS BOOKS WHAT I SAW. Death is both male and female hence female death is the one to sit at the gate of hell and receive her wicked and evil children. (Eve). They must tell her that they love her upon entry into hell. Hence death deals in love but Good God and Allelujah deal in truth – true love.

I've told you about the charcoal full black moon that I saw. Hence the death of man woman and children including beasts; animals will be global. We've caused humanity, billions in humanity to become extinct without even knowing it.

Yes I saw the little moon about one quarter (1/4) the size of a full moon but this moon is for Good God's Children and people and not all in humanity. We are not all his children and that's truly a shame.

YOU CANNOT KILL AND DO ALL THAT IS WRONG – EVIL AND THINK YOU ARE GOING TO GET INTO GOOD GOD AND ALLELUJAH'S ABODE. YOU WILL BE REJECTED AND BILLIONS ARE REJECTED BECAUSE THEY LIVE TO KILL AND TELL LIES ON LIFE – HIM GOOD GOD AND ALLELUJAH. And the sad part of this is, we teach our children these same lies. If truth is everlasting life, why not live for truth and live? Why tell lies and die to go to hell? Come on now.

Some of us live to break the law and laws of Good God and Allelujah whilst others say he does not exist. So if he Good God and Allelujah do not exist, why are you here? Why is humanity here?

Did we just pop out of the air and existed?

Some are just plain out ignorant that refuse to hear the truth. And yes some of us teach our children in the like manner of our ignorance and stupidity.

Some become fools as well as educated fools. Hence they live for death including capturing our soul and or spirit and send it straight to hell. Hence the spirit and or soul catchers in the physical realm; demons that walk and talk on the earth literally.

So when we are like this, what can he Good God and Allelujah do to save us; me and you? We do not truly belong to him. We belong to death and his slated to go to hell and die shortly, hence the full charcoal black moon.

He Good God and Allelujah have to leave you to the decision you have made.

❖ *Killing is a choice that hundreds of millions, no billions make.*

❖ *Stealing is a choice that hundreds of millions if not billions make.*

❖ *Adultery is a choice that hundreds of millions if not billions make.*

❖ *Going against the law and laws of Good God and Allelujah is a choice we all make.*

❖ *Marrying the wrong person is a choice we make.*

❖ *Having wicked and evil children is a choice we all make and made because none of us asked him Good God and Allelujah for true, right, just, honest, clean and truly loving children that will not follow in the way evil but walk in the righteousness and integrity of all that is positive and true.*

The bad and or wrong choices we made and make have consequences. We are the ones that must now bare the pain. We listened to WICKED AND EVIL PEOPLE LIE TO US AND NOW WE MUST PAY THE PRICE LIKE EVE (EVENING) AND DIE.

<u>Listen, if Good God and Allelujah is saying this is wrong do don't follow the wrong and or folly ground. Truly listen because it's your life he's saving. He knows the death of hell and the fire you are going to face. So why die? Why not live for life and truly live?</u> Why not listen to him (Good God and Allelujah) for a change and truly save yourself. Hey, you may say I am a nut job and need help whether psychiatric or spiritual, but it matters not to me what you think of me negatively. At the end of the day, I delivered the message of him and her Good God and Allelujah. It's up to you to reject the message or accept the message. Like I've said in another book, my soul and spirit (spiritual energy and body) is secure with Good God and Allelujah and I infinitely and indefinitely forever ever more than infinite and indefinite lifetimes and generations infinitely do not need yours (your soul and spirit) nor do I want it. Save yourself. I've told you, Good God and Allelujah cannot save you if you do not belong to him. So if you are truly not Jewish, truly good luck to you because you truly have no chance in hell to be saved. Meaning if you are not walking in the way of truth, truly good luck to you.

He Good God does not want to see anything bad happen to you so why not listen to him and obey his laws?

WHY LET WICKED AND EVIL PEOPLE TAKE YOU TO HELL WITH THEM? Come on now. This is your life and it is important no matter the stress, heartache and pain you feel and or you are under.

As a youth if you know certain things are wrong, don't do it. A FRIENDSHIP IS NOT WORTH LOSING YOUR SOUL AND OR LIFE FOR AND OR OVER.

A TRUE FRIEND WOULD NEVER JEOPARDIZE YOUR LIFE FOR NAUGHT – A PLACE IN HELL. COME ON NOW.

Well he's my bonafide, my homey and I have to ride with him. It's ride or die. Then die because your bonafide and homey has and have chosen death for you. He or she did not choose life.

Like I said, a true friend would not jeopardize your life and you would not jeopardize his or hers either.

LISTEN, IT'S EASY TO GO TO HELL BUT IT'S NOT EASY TO GET OUT OF HELL. In all my travels in the spiritual realm, I'VE YET TO SEE ANYONE ESCAPE HELL. So truly good luck to many of you that are waiting for a saving grace to redeem your life. And truly good luck to many of you that have chosen the path of death.

Truly good luck to many of you who have tattooed the names of your homeys on your skin - body because that dead homey can take your life in the living.

Truly good luck to many of you who are in gangs and or follow your homey to hell - grave of and or home of death; the dead. Too late is your cry and will forever be your cry literally. It's amazing how Good God has been trying to protect us from hell and we keep going into the fire; can't leave it alone. The heat of the sun is nothing compared to the fire and or heat that is going to burn your spirit. Let's put it this way. The heat of the sun is like cold and or ice compared to the heat that is going to burn your spirit. So if it has not been said to you in the living you will hear it upon death and that message will say, Joanna, Carla, Samantha, Richard, Tyrone, Trayvon, Travis, Beulah, Tammy, Ricardo, Santana, Carlos, Edwardo, Jessepie, Carlo welcome to hell. _**The names are for example and or reference only people.**_

Like I've said and will say again, **_THE LIFE YOU LIVE IN THE LIVING (PHYSICAL) DETERMINES WHERE YOU GO IN SPIRITUAL._** So if you live an evil life in the living you are going to go to hell and burn. There are no ands ifs or buts about this. Your sins outweigh your good hence you are hell bound. See instructions for death if you have not read this book to see if you are on death's list. You need to know the sins you have done in your lifetime as well because the sins of your mother and father, grandparents and past generations also affect you. And before I go on I am going to interrupt this book again. It's August 27, 2014 and I just dreamt about Tatum Channing. I can't remember the dream which is weird because it was so vivid. Yes I've been forgetting more and more but it's weird because I am dreaming about water and young children more and more. I am not sure if the water is destructive. I just have to watch and see because I truly cannot tell you the land I am seeing the water in. But this is not what I wanted to tell you. I am seeing faces more and more again. Hence I wish I was an artist that could draw the faces of the people that I am seeing. Listen I can only give you a vague description of the people that I am seeing. Just this morning I saw this young white boy. I would peg him to be 18 – 24 if not younger. He had brown hair and a roundish nose not straight. He was not fat nor was he too skinny. His eyes were closed and he was in ice water frozen. The water around him was a bit cloudy not murky. I guess frosty would be a better description of the water. I can't remember if he had on a blue grey suit, but he was not shabbily dressed hence I would associate his attire with a function. The week before that I saw this light and or brown skinned black man that was medium built before me. I can't describe his clothing or give you a better description of him because he truly won't let me although I can see is face. He had low cut hair and I am sorry I cannot give you a better description than this. It is the best I can do. As for the young white boy in the icy water, parents truly take heed and warn your child and or children to stay away from icy water especially if they are going to have a function. This young man did not look poor. Warn your child and or children about drinking and getting drunk in the winter season. Listen, I do not comprehend the faces I see before me when I am awake nor do I know the lands they are in. All I can do is warn you and try to describe the faces I am seeing to the best of my ability. Taking drawing course is something I may have to do to capture these faces but in truth I really and truly don't want to. I truly do not want to see death's faces on paper. Have these people died yet?

No, hence sometimes you can save the living and or people in the living if you know how to. My descriptions are vague but like I said, this is the best I can do.

ONWARDS I GO

But Jesus said, he is the way and the light and anyone that believe in him will be saved and or have everlasting life. And please forgive me if I get the wording and or quote wrong. *TRUTH IS; A MAN CANNOT SAVE YOU IF HE KNOWS YOU NOT. NOR CAN HE SAVE YOU IF HE IS NOT ORDAINED TO DO SO; SAVE YOU. HENCE MANY OF YOU WILL HEAR TOO LATE AND I KNOW YOU NOT IN THE GRAVE.*

If I don't know you nor am I ordained to save you, how can I save you? I cannot.

And don't even go there with the seeds he Good God and Allelujah has and have given me. Good God knows the truth and goodness of these people hence he's given them to me. I have to truly get to know them and they have to get to know me. These people are Good God's saving grace and I am to help them; save them. They are the ones that can save many of you with the good that they do.

If he Good God has not given you to me I cannot save you, no one can. HENCE KNOW YOUR SINS AND

THE BOOK YOUR NAME IS WRITTEN IN. Death hath time and sin used the time death had to reduce humanity to rubble. Humanity sinned reckless and rude and forgot that "THE WAGES OF SIN IS DEATH."

As parents we say our children are a blessing but yet if they were a blessing to us, why are we screwing them up and messing up their lives and future?

Why are we locking them out of GOOD GOD AND ALLELUJAH'S KINGDOM?

You don't truly love your child because you readily hand them over to sin – death in the long run. Instead of saving them you kill them.

If Good God forbids you to do something then stay away from that something. Islam is not clean and he Good God and Allelujah has and have forbidden his children to go into this religion and way of life. This way of life is the Babylonian Way of life now and we cannot accept it. We have to leave this way alone. We can no longer live like SOLOMON who did not listen to Good God and Allelujah. If Good God say do not do something then truly don't do it because he knows what he's talking about. Solomon disobeyed and paid the price – cost. So truly don't be like him. As Good God's children and people we are to live in the like manner of Psalms One. We are not to walk in the council of the ungodly – wicked and vile. We know this but yet we are walking in the council's of the ungodly as well as doing the ills and or wrongs of the ungodly.

As Good God's children and people we are not to marry anyone Islamic nor are we to go into their land or lands and bask in their offerings. Good God specifically told us to stay away from these people because they say life and call on the Breath of Life but yet they kill life; kill the Breath of Life.

Nothing Babylonian is good hence they were separated from us long ago. Evil cannot change so I truly do not know why we would or could think that we can change evil. Evil is XX and please do not associate X or XX with females and or the female gene. Evil is white hence white cannot change it must be white forever ever. So White stays the same in the physical and spiritual realm because white is of both worlds –realm. Meaning White is in the spirit. If you are confused, go to the internet and pull up a picture of the Ying and Yang, this will explain things perfectly.

And for this pending race war that everyone is gearing up for, it has to stop. A young child should not have to stop me and ask me what colour I am. Yes I have white blood in me but that does not define who I am as a person. In truth I am so sick of the light skinned dark skinned bullshit that is happening. Listen ignorant and daft people. Enough with the skin and or hue bullshit because I truly do not give a rat's ass about hue – colour of skin. No we are not all a part of the human race and I refuse to let anyone put me in a damned bracket based on hue; colour of skin. Bleep you when you do this. THE COLOUR OF MY SKIN DOES NOT DEFINE ME NOR DOES IT DEFINE MY CHARACTER AS A PERSON AND HUMAN BEING.

I AM NOT DEFINED BY SOCIETY, I AM DEFINED BY ME, THE PERSON I AM AND THE GOOD AND TRUE LIFE THAT I LIVE.

Take you light skinned and dark skinned bullshit and shove it up your ass. No for real. Why should I fall in a bracket because you put me in one? Do not put me in any of your psychological messed up and demented brackets. I DO NOT NEED A PLACE TO BELONG BECAUSE I HAVE ONE WITH GOOD GOD AND ALLELUJAH ALREADY AND THIS PLACE IS INFINITELY AND INDEFINITELY FINE BY ME AS WELL AS SUIT ME.

I am so tired of hearing of biracial people don't belong. I am neither black nor white and no side accept me. Bleep all of you who think this way. You f-ing belong to the black race but that choice is up to you. Bleep all of you too if you are saying you don't belong. Who the fuck cares!!! I certainly don't. I do not let colour define me and fuck the black and white race if they don't accept me. As long as Good God and Allelujah accept me and the goodness that I try to do and do, then I am infinitely and indefinitely good to go. IF YOU BELONG ALREADY, WHY ARE YOU LISTENING TO PEOPLE TELL YOU YOU DON'T BELONG? Accept you for who you are because at the end of the day, race cannot get you in Good God and Allelujah's kingdom and or abode. I will not be grouped and put in any and absolutely no one can tell me that I am not black because I fall under the banner of black, was born under the banner of life – black, descended from the banner of blue; spiritual life (black) hence I have life all around. THE COLOUR OF SKIN DOES NOT MAKE YOU BLACK NOR DOES IT MAKE YOU WHITE IT JUST MAKES YOU DEAD – SINFUL. We as human beings are the ones to define each other by skin colour; hue. At the end of the day when all is said and done, we are going to have to shed hue – physical and spiritual hue anyway. So keep your colour bullshit and don't come to me with it because I will put all your ignorant and daft asses in your place. When you truly know about life then truly come and talk to me but for now keep your racist, based on skin tone bigotry to your damned self. Don't need it because I refuse it. As long as he Good God and Allelujah give me his blessing and permission to be with someone, I am going to be with that person. Fuck what you think because that person is well given. And no he would not give me a Babylonian or a German because I refuse them period. And no this is not based on race but based on deeds – sins.

As humans we accepted the Babylonians and their dirty idols and religion and think it would not cost us and it did cost us.

We are the ones to think that the Babylonian Way is okay when it is truly not. The Babylonian Way cost Eve because she died. She lost everything including her place with Good God and Allelujah so what makes any of us think differently; that it would not cost us our lives as well?

Humanity is slated to die before 2032 and this is our own doing. This is our extinction, the extinction of wicked and evil people including children. And if your child is not wicked and evil and you are, your child is going to die because your sins fall on your children also. Meaning, if you cannot and or did not pay your debt with death, death can and will take your child and or children.

We allowed them (the Babylonians) to pollute our way and now look at the black nations and people that have accepted this way of life, religion and living today.

- ❖ *They've become scavengers like them*
- ❖ *Murderers like them*
- ❖ *Liars and deceivers like them*

- ❖ *Adulterers like them*
- ❖ *Thieves like them*
- ❖ *Spiritually and physically poor like them*
- ❖ *Dead like them*
- ❖ *Without a home like them*
- ❖ *Locked out of Good God and Allelujah's kingdom and or abode like them.*
- ❖ *Barren and hopeless just like them*

Good God and Allelujah specifically told me my homeland Jamaica is unclean. I cannot go back to the island, no one can until Jamaica becomes clean. They have a saving grace. They can save themselves but I truly do not trust them to change their dirty ways. Yes this is sad on my part. THEY MADE A PLEDGE; VOW TO HIM GOOD GOD AND ALLELUJAH AND THEY COULD NOT HONOUR IT. And like the majority of humanity we broke our pledge and or vow of truth to him Good God and Allelujah also. Our pledge of truth is like unto a marriage vow. No it's not like unto a marriage vow, it is our marriage vow and we are to honour it. Yes we've all made a pledge to Good God and Allelujah and none, not one of us could honour it. Hence we've all failed him including me because I too have sinned. But with all this said, he Good God and Allelujah has never given up on us nor did he give up on me. We are the ones to give up on him and accept the false teachings and lies of the Babylonians – death's true children.

Once again, no matter what the Islamic Community say, and no matter how they set me up to die, he Good God and Allelujah will never fail me because it is him that I truly love and adore as well as trust over anyone in humanity. He shows me your wicked and evil nature; ways as well as plots before they happen. Hence I leave every Muslim globally to him Good God and Allelujah – Time because I know the death in time for every wicked and evil people including child (ren).

Hell is your home and in time you will reach it because "the wages (pay) of sin is death." And no one can escape death if their name is written in the book of sin; the dead.

Good God never told any of us to kill – take life to see him.

He gave us life so why would he take it from us? Humans are giver backer takers not Good God and Allelujah. Come on now. We take life and expect him Good God and Allelujah to reward us for our lies; sins and or disobedience including the lives we've taken.

Wey unnu tek Gad fa? Come on now. Sin not and keep the law and laws of Good God and Allelujah and live. Come on now.

Satan is a giver backer taker because all he's given you he wants it back and he does take it back in some way.

It matters not how he takes it back because some of you are alcoholics.

❖ *Some of you are murders hence your multiple prison terms and bouts with the law.*

❖ *Some of you are drug addicts hence all you work for go into drugs and many of you lose it all including wife and children; lovely and happy home.*

❖ *Some of you become prostitutes for the CEO's and CFO's of the company you work for. Hence many of you give up your lives and or souls for them with the contract you've signed.*

❖ *Some of you, your children must prostitute themselves for them. Hence the young child prostitutes that are on television whoring themselves for the dollar bill. They sell sex and promiscuity and there isn't a damned thing the government and sensors can do about it because they condone bullshit like this. Are company owned. Lay in wait like prostitutes and dogs for their tax dollar and hand out.*

Many of us see the nastiness of the Islamic and Christian world and condone this. Say it's okay but it's not okay. We are disrespecting God and Self. Come on now. Why the hell should you and your children die for a place in hell? What right do any of you have to sacrifice self to death? What right? And yes I am yelling. Life is given live it because Good God gave none of us sickness nor did he give us death. Sometimes he will make us sick for us not to go to a certain place or event he does not approve of. So truly know how he is trying to save you. I know he's trying to save me from my homeland hence he took me out long ago. Decades ago because he knew just how dirty and filthy my land and people would become. Yes I see people going back home and I yearn to go just like them but it's LIFE OVER DEATH I SAY. I have to stay loyal and true to Good God and Allelujah because he's loyal and true to me. Hence I have to stay put in all that I do until he sends me on that well deserved vacation real soon.

So how can children be the future when we readily hand them over to death; hell to burn.

How the hell can we say we love our children and let them die?

Damn I forgot you love and cannot truly love. Hence death's children must tell her they love her upon entering hell because it's love that screw up our lives and send us to hell to die. Love screwed Eve and or Hawwah, hence love took all from her and killed her.

We are the ones to refuse to listen to Good God.

We are the ones to listen to others and mess up our lives.

HE COOD GOD AND ALLELUJAH TOLD YOU SPECIFICALLY NOT TO TRUST BABYLON. NOT BECAUSE OF SKIN COLOUR BUT BECAUSE THEY ARE LIARS AND THIEVES AND THEY ARE NOT OF HIM, NOR DO THEY LIKE HIM. BUT NOOOOOOOOOOOO WE COULD NOT LISTEN. WE REFUSE TO LISTEN AND LOOK AT HUMANITY TODAY.

Your lands are so infested with Babylonians that you look up to them. And you the nasty black race take it further by throwing your wonderful hair of truth – electricity and buy their nasty weaves (human so called hair). Your hair is electric – electromagnetic energy that shrinks when water touch it. But when braided, not in corn row – the ends – your hair stand up at night. Yes go up to Good God and Allelujah for truth, praise; life.

You're all a fucking disgrace to the black and human race. No wonder they can call you slaves – Abdullah. Servants to them but Slaves in the true sense. And don't go there because I did tell you in another book I told my son he can take Abdullah out of his name but because of respect for his grandmother he choose to leave Abdullah in his name and I have to respect him for that. I know he Good God and Allelujah will not sin him or cause him to be sinned, hence death cannot hold him down and charge him for sin when it comes his name. He spoke the truth of his desire hence I have to respect him, Death and Good God and Allelujah have to respect him for that.

"TRUTH IS EVERLASTING LIFE," hence it is wise to be truthful all the time.

As youths you have a choice to do good or evil. Good is the better choice over evil. Yes I know we all say it doesn't pay to be good. But trust me it pays to do good. You may not see your goodness today but Good God and Allelujah see it. Hence you are rewarded with life in his abode. And in truth you will see your goodness tomorrow; months and years from now.

There is a life and death (Ying and Yang) but that life is up to you. YOU ARE YOUR OWN DECISION MAKER. YOU ARE ALSO YOUR OWN HELL MAKER. So truly live clean and good because no one wants to go to hell.

We all say this; we don't want to go to hell but yet NONE OF US LIVE CLEAN, meaning try our best not to go to hell.

We know the fires of hell and ignore it.

We know that the wages of sin is death but yet ignore this law.

So how are we going to be saved if we've abandoned the law and laws of Good God and Allelujah?

Tell me something, can a man save himself if does not know how to?

Tell me this yet again. Why are we listening to Babylonians and or wicked and evil people that can't save us and or care not about us? Their saving grace is hell, so why want to go to hell with them and burn?

Why lose your soul and or place with Good God and Allelujah for people who care not about you?

I know some parents don't care either hence many teach and preach wrong. My children do wrong and I tell them, even see the danger before it happens but some truly don't listen; hence their hurt and pain is their hurt and pain not mine. You are taking them out of the fire but they don't want a saving grace; want to come out the fire. They want to go into the fire and get burned.

If I am telling you there is fire over there don't go there and you push to go there, when the fire burns you I will not be there to help you. I am going to leave you in the fire and this is basically what he Good God and Allelujah has and have done to us. He keeps taking us out of the fire and we keep running back into it. He's tired now. Hence he's left us to the decision we've made. He's burnt out and tired of talking to people – children that refuse to listen.

He keeps telling us the fire of hell is hot don't walk the road of sin because you are going to die. He's constantly been doing this and we are the ones to not listen. So because he's tired of trying with stiff necked and hard ears people, he went his own way and left us to our desires – sins; death.

We do not want life so he must move on and go forward. Move on and save those who want and need him – life. He knew our death in time and he did try to save us but instead of listening to good and true council, we listened to death and now billions are slated to die and this is unfortunate.

WE MADE THE CHOICE OF DEATH. SO DEATH MUST NOW TAKE US – ALL WHO CHOSE HIM.

We cannot say we love God and go against him like that.

We cannot say we care but yet turn around and break his law and laws – disobey him. We stabbed him in the back and wonder why he's here with us. We are the ones to hurt him, so why should he constantly be around people that hurt him all the time?

We cannot say we love our children and then turn around and give them death. You felt the labour pains; contraction pains. So tell me with all this pain you feel, why turn your child and or children over to sin; death? You truly did not love that child then. Come on now.

My children give me trouble until this day, and I have a mandate of November 1, 2014 to leave their ass but I still pray for them. I take my complaints to him Good

God and Allelujah. When I leave are they going to feel it?

Not all but some. When you have a good parent and or good parents including grandparents and friends that truly love you, cherish them and do good and well by them because they are doing well and good by you. True and good friends including family members are hard to find hence truly hold on to the good and true ones that you have. Respect them because despite your failures they too can save you in the end.

A wicked person will never try to save you. They will always try to destroy and kill you, meaning do all to take you to hell with them by any means necessary.

EVIL DOES NOT LIKE LONELY BECAUSE EVIL KNOWS NOT THE COMFORT IN SOLITUDE – TRUTH.

EVIL KNOWS NOT QUIET HENCE EVERYTHING HAVE TO BE LOUD, NOISY.

When things are loud and noisy you cannot hear Good God and Allelujah nor can you communicate with him. Your mind is distracted hence evil will and or the negative side of our mind will jump in and distract you from reaching him Good God and Allelujah. And many of you know what I am talking about hence calm and slow down the chatter in the mind. Bad chatter that is.

As a mother you cannot feel the pain and or go throw so much for 10 months plus and just hand over your child and or children to death just like that. Why send your child to hell and burn? Use the 28 day calendar to calculate a woman's pregnancy term.

Why cause them pain?

Tell me something, did you just have children to just hand dem ova to death jus suh?

Did some of you just have children to laugh at them while they burn in hell's fire?

Some of you are saying no I did not. Then the question I ask you yet again is. Why hand your child and or children over to death? And please do not use the church as an excuse because we all know the churches of the world rob us of life all around. We as humans are the ones to choose these churches hoping to find God when he Good God and Allelujah resides in us. We are both physical and spiritual beings with the spirit being a reflection of the flesh and the flesh is a reflection of the spirit. Both work hand in hand hence they are both the same in a lot of ways. Yes there are differences but those differences are minute, meaning you as a fleshy being cannot truly tell the difference. You do not know where to look hence you cannot find the differences. We all know Good God did not tell any of us to go into whore houses (churches) to kill ourselves. Not one church globally can say they stand for Good God and Allelujah nor can any say they represent him. Every church globally represents death and the devil hence WHITE AND BLACK DEATH (JESUS) is sold globally.

It's amazing how we say we love our children but as soon as death and his wicked and evil people come along we say, here you go death you can have my child as a sacrifice unto you.

Death did not feel the pain you did. So why hand your child and or children willingly over to death? Come on now.

What right do any of you have to do this?

Did your child and or children say, mom dad sacrifice me? I will go to hell and burn for you. I will be like the Babylonians and walk on fire, even worship fire, the cow for you. None did this. So why the hell are you sacrificing your own?

When did Good God and Allelujah say, make sacrifices unto me?

When did he tell us to kill self to see him?

When did he tell us to kill and or sacrifice our children to see him?

Death is a sin not a right nor is it life.

Now tell me something. Is your child's life worth nothing to you?

No don't answer that because I can. Your child's life mean nothing to you hence you sacrifice them unto the wicked, wicked and evil beings including demons that can't wait to inflict pain on them in front of your eyes.

KNOW THIS. IF YOU DID NOT WANT CHILDREN YOU SHOULD HAVE FOUND A MAN OR WOMAN THAT DID NOT WANT TO HAVE ANY. YOU SHOULD HAVE KEPT YOURSELF PURE UNTIL THE DAY COMES WHEN DEATH'S TIME IS UP AND DEATH IS NO MORE TO HAVE CHILDREN. ONCE DEATH'S TIME IS UP HAVE GOOD AND TRUE, POSITIVE AND CLEAN CHILDREN WITH GOOD GOD AND ALLELUJAH.

REMEMBER THE BABYLONIANS HAVE ALWAYS SACRIFICED THEIR CHILDREN'S LIFE UNTO THEIR GODS. So why are you following them?

If they can hand guns and ammunition to their children and say kill why are you practicing and worshipping including living like them and for them?

IF THEY BREAK EVERY COMMANDMENT OF GOOD GOD AND ALLELUJAH WHY ARE YOU FOLLOWING THEM? Why are you emulating them? They mock your god and tell lies on him. So why walk in the way of them or even let them in your land (s) – home?

Good God has and have blessed me with his truth and one of the things I've asked him for is: I want no Babylonian of any kind in our new kingdom and abode infinitely and indefinitely more than forever ever without end. I truly do not need them, nor do I need their idol worship and lies. I need honesty and true peace because I am trying to make my life truly honest and peaceful where I don't have to be nor want and need to be around wicked and evil people; them. I truly love Good God and Allelujah hence I have to find a safe haven that is pure and void of all sins for us both; him and me including his children and people. Satan and or the devil can keep every disobedient child and or people. Don't need disobedience and non listeners around me. I need to be stress free and contented with my Lovey hence freedom from this controlled and evil system of things is a must for me and the ones that truly love me and Good God. Wicked and evil people including the Babylonians do not like Good God and Allelujah hence they do all to fight against goodness and truth – Good God; him. They the Babylonians including wicked and evil children and people disobey Good God and Allelujah and withhold the truth from humanity. So why would I want them in our new kingdom. Truly look into things. We say we have 10 commandments of God and that's a lie, there are more than ten. Count them and you will see. But with these ten commandments that we say is from God, we do not obey them, nor do we respect any of them because we break them daily. So if we break the commandments of God daily, why should he stick around and help us? And why would he want us in his kingdom and or home; abode? Are we not telling him Good God and Allelujah that we do not respect him nor do we respect his law and laws?

SO WHY SHOULD HE SAVE US IF WE CAN'T OBEY HIM; WE ARE DISOBEDIENT?

The god of Babylon and the people of Babylon are not my god and people and will never ever be my god and people. Hence keep the gods and people of Babylon the hell out of my kingdom; that which I have with Good God and Allelujah. Don't come wanting any of our goodness nor beg any of our goodness because none will be

extended to you. Let your decrepit god and gods feed your asses and provide for you. There is no sharing game here. Your god is your god and mine is mine hence let me keep mine and live whilst you keep yours and die. You don't know my God so why should I help to feed you? Why the hell would I disrespect mine (my god) and give you a helping hand when you truly don't know mine (my god) nor do you care about him? Let the god of your choosing feed and clothe you; even shelter you. The olive branch will never be extended hence I ask Good God and Allelujah to let all I do; help good and clean people, trying people that are good and true that need help. Good people that are going through the struggle and still holding on to him like me. My food and water is my food and water as well as their food and water. Good God gave it to me hence I refuse to share it with any of you (wicked and evil people). You do not know goodness so why should I be good to you? I am going to pass you by because all you did and do in your life is wicked and evil things, hence goodness must not help nor come into contact with evil; wicked and evil people. Come on now. All you did was for evil and now that evil has abandoned you, you are looking for a helping hand from good. You should have thought about all the people you hurt; killed, kept down in your life of evil. You did all manner of evil and good is to turn the other cheek and say, its okay. Hell to the F-ing No. Stay the bleep being evil because I truly want or need nothing to do with you. I will however gladly share this food and water with Good God and Allelujah's children and people, but I will never ever share any with you and he Good God cannot make me share with you. Trust me I will remind him of your evils and your disrespect. I respect him so why would I be like the foolish ones and help evil? Evil cannot change (XX) but XY can change. (Not based on genes or genetics so please do not use genes and genetics here (male and female). I know some of you are tempted to do this. Know that the XX and XY have different meanings depending on your level of spirituality, but in the case and or terms of evil, XX cannot change). Good God's blessings is our blessings so let your god, the god of your choice bless you. Not even a drop of water will I give to you hence he Good God and Allelujah know to separate us infinitely and indefinitely forever ever without end. We will keep our good and true, clean and positive borders away from the lots of you as well. Don't want to see you or even know that you exist. My

God and Friend, Lovey is taking care of us hence we will indefinitely forever ever without end keep our blessings and him. And it matters not if you are Chinese, Black, White or Indian Babylonian including Spiritual Babylonian, none of you, not one of you are welcomed in Good God and Allelujah's new kingdom with me. None of you can reside there forever ever without end.

THE SIGN READS: NO TRESPASSING, NO STRAGLERS, NO STRAYS, ABSOLUTELY NO BABYLONIAN OF ANY KIND, SO TRULY TAKE HEED. Where no bones are provided, no dogs are invited.

We know the law and laws of Good God and Allelujah. They are simple and basic but yet we refuse them, and when the devil and the demons of hell beat us up; we are running back to him Good God and Allelujah. For what? Why run back? Stay with your choice. Come on now. And for many of you it's too late, truly too late. So why sin and do wrong in the first place?

If we as humans truly loved him Good God WE WOULD TURN THE DEVIL AND HIS CHIDLREN AWAY BUT WE REFUSE TO DO THAT.

<u>We say they are with us. How the hell can</u>
<u>someone be with you if they give you death</u>
<u>and tell you to go against your god, people</u>
<u>and land?</u>

<u>If that person truly cared and truly loved you, they</u>
<u>would not tell you to dishonour and disrespect your</u>
<u>god. HENCE NOT ALL IN HUMANITY BELONGS</u>
<u>TO GOD – GOOD GOD AND ALLELUJAH, THEY</u>
<u>BELONG TO SIN AND DEATH.</u>

If you had truly loved and respected Good God then you would not let others tell you to disrespect him. You would have passed over death. You would have said to death's children; "I have my god already and he suits me just fine. Please remember my door number and tell others of your kind not to knock at my door giving me their religious bullshit – garbage."

"But my god can save you."

"No he cannot. Your god did not create the heavens and the earth. Your god did not make and or create the waters of the earth, nor did he plant the seeds in the earth to grow so that earth can maintain, sustain as well as feed us."

"But my god is the god of all."

"Well if he's the god of all, why are you at my door selling him to me? Should I not know him also? All that is good and of him I should know hence I would be with him. But because your god is not my god and you have to sell your god and his hate; lies. You tell lies on my wonderful and beautiful friend, bunnunoonus God therefore I know not your god. And for the record, Good God and Allelujah is not the god of all because it is said in your holy book that he "God put enmity between his seed and thy seed (the devil's seed)" and because I know for a fact and without a shadow of a doubt more than infinitely and indefinitely that my God would never ever forever ever never ever put enmity (strife) and hatred between anyone, I leave your god to time as well as the hell hole he's carved out for himself. Your god and his lies is hell bound and this is guaranteed. Hence I truly do not want or need your god. Keep your lying and deceiving devil of a god. Your god is a warmonger and trouble maker; a god of hate and strife and I truly do not want or need him. My God is of peace, true peace hence he's the truth; he's life and not death. Please do not come back to my door selling me death because I pass over death. I truly love my god and true friend more than so. He's dear to me and he's my forever ever life. So please do not get me to disrespect him hence you will not like the consequences of hell. I do not come to your door selling my God and never will because he cannot be bought or sold. I know him and I know the good and true life he's given me and I am keeping it no matter my hurt and pain because I know this pain is but for a time."

"But if your god truly loved you he will not let you feel pain."

"Sir, my pain is not caused by my God, it is caused by Man and the evils that they do. Wicked and people like you that is trying to get me to leave my god. My stress and pain is caused by wicked and evil people like you; the wickedness that you do for me to fall. My stress and pain is caused by wicked and evil people in my workplace that seek for me to lose my job so that I can't feed my children whilst ending up in the streets. Wicked and evil people like you that will do all for me to put death over life and I refuse to do this. I refuse to put death over life because death did not give me life, life did. I have to stay true to life because its life I see with me in my struggles. Its life that held on to me when death came knocking at my door. So why should I be ungrateful to him. I have him (life) already I do not need or want death. So please do not give me your lies because I am definitely not Eve (Evening). I will defend my god and territory so step off and leave. Know that this Lyon (s) will trample you down and devour you. So truly don't when it comes to me and my true love; God. I have all I need in him and I will not give it up for naught; you and your God. You are Satan in disguise hence I will not be fooled by you."

"But my god can give you all. All you have to do is believe in him."

"I don't believe in my God. I know my God hence the big difference between me and you. Given the right opportunity and if another god come along you will give up your god to join another church and or congregation; god. I don't have to do that with mine. He's my rock and shied hence he's my true protector against villains of deceit and corruption like you. Know that one day all evil must come to an end and soon very soon it will end. The blood water that is happening on earth is a tell tale sign, the sink holes, earthquakes and tsunami's of earth are all tell tale signs. The full charcoal black moon, the fire in the sky, the full moon of fire are all tell tale signs. Hence those that have accepted death have no chance in hell to escape death and hell. I know my god hence I praise him and give him thanks for the good and the bad. I know to live my life clean, good and true. You don't because if you did you would not be standing here selling me death. Good day sir and may your God truly have mercy on your soul for the lies you tell on him or her. My God is not your god because if he was you wouldn't be telling lies on him and selling him. Good day Judas because hell is truly your home." And he closed his door and went inside. Father God truly have mercy on those who tell lies on you as well as spread lies on you because they truly do not know what they have done. Truly have mercy on them because the Ark is here and all whose name is not written in your book of life will surely die. Hence I ask again, how can people say they love you but readily tell lies on you?"

How can people say they care but yet send others to hell to die with them? I truly love you hence you are my grace and mercy; true truth and life. I will not forsake you nor leave you hence I leave my enemies in your hands. All that knowing and truly hurt you I leave in your hands to their own hell. You've never lied on any of us so why should we turn around and lie to you and on you? Life; true life isn't death hence I choose life at all times forever ever without end over death. Like I said, you are my good keep and I truly love you no matter my trials and tribulations; pain. I know death is time and it is in time and for a time, but soon death will be no more and life in time will be secure; rein forever more. Life; the truth must prevail; hence I wait patiently on you because death has and have reached that point in time when they must take their own infinitely and indefinitely forever ever without end forevermore.

I look to you hence you are my strength, my all; Allelujah; true breath of life.

My prayer has gone up now. Let thy good will be done Allelujah because in truth you gave us truth, all that is good and true, we as humans were the ones to give up you and all the goodness you've given us for lies and deceit, the wages of sin which is death.

Not one of us can blame you for our demise because you did not give us religions of men to kill self or anyone. We were the ones to accept lies and say they

are of you and from you when we knew they were of death and not of you or from you.

We were the ones to forget that evil – the devil as we call him was going to use any means necessary to sway us as well as convince us; man and humanity to leave you as well as deceive you.

We forgot that evil will never ever like good. Hence evil do all and give us all to distract us as well as disrespect our god – you Good God and Allelujah.

We forgot lies to the devil and or wicked and evil people are the truth hence lying comes natural to them. Their lies are convincing and if you do not know the truth, you will get caught up in their lies and mess and this is what has happened to humanity today. All that you Good God tell us not to do we do. We are the ones to believe in the Jesus lie and this is sad. The lie did not work for Eve (Evening) hence it will not work for you; us. We know the wages of sin is death and Jesus cannot change this because he too is death, hence we are told to die to see god. And I've told you; the people of the world; humanity, no one can die to see Good God and Allelujah. You can only die to see death. Now if your mind can stomach it, look at a dead body. Does that body have life?

No right?

So why want to be this way, dead and or die? Death has no life and you see this so why not live for life and live? Come on now. No one can sin and be okay. Each and every one of us know the lie but we've forgotten about it. Hence humanity; man including women and children became sin's greatest weapon(s) against him Good God and Allelujah. Sin was victorious over man – humanity because all the sins we do; commit globally on a daily basis over the years and century's humanity truly cannot repay. Hence the sins of the fathers and mothers, forefathers and mothers follow us from generation unto generation. Not one of us chose life hence we've become the first begotten of the dead; death; the children of death. Not one of us say let me do all the good I can do and wipe the slate of my ancestors, forefathers and mothers clean and this is truly sad.

But you don't do that for your homeland you are saying. I do despite me stepping aside and not trusting them. I still push Jamaica because I truly know the God I have. Despite my tears he did hear me and gave Jamaica a chance to come clean. The ball and water is in their court. Meaning it's up to them to truly come clean and live. Not one drop of human blood must be spilt on the land. All the evils that they do must infinitely and indefinitely stop forever ever without end. Despite me taking the flag of life from them and handing it back to Good God and Allelujah they can get it back. And like I said, it's up to them. They have to secure themselves as well as secure the future of their children and grandchildren even great grandchildren. If I could save all of Jamaica I would but I would never ever save the wicked and evil people of the land because I know the hurt and pain of evil. Evil belongs to death and I would never ever take an evil person from death. Yes you can say I am hateful and spiteful and all I have to say is who feels it knows it. I know physical and spiritual wickedness hence if I am the saving grace for humanity, I truly would never save a wicked and evil person including child. I refuse to because in all of their wickedness and evil, they did not think of the hurt and pain they were causing the next person and or Good God. They did not think of the goodness of life, so why the hell should I have mercy and compassion on any of them. Life is worth it hence we have to work hard at it in order to live. We have to stay focused and true despite our hurt and pain. HENCE I DEDICATE LIFE WE LIVE BY JAH CURE TO HIM GOOD GOD AND ALLELUJAH AND ALL THE GOOD AND TRYING PEOPLE OF THIS WORLD INCLUDING CHILD. NEVER GIVE UP BECAUSE SOON AND VERY SOON WICKED PEOPLE SHALL BE NO MORE. THIS I GUARANTEE THUS SAITH THE LORD THY GOD MEANING IT IS SO. TRULY TRUST AND REST YOUR SHOULDER ON GOOD GOD AND LET HIM

TAKE YOU THROUGH. YES YOU WILL SLIP AND FALL BUT PICK YOURSELF UP AND KEEP GOING BECAUSE YOU ARE TRULY BLESSED AND HIGHLY FAVOURED. NEVER FORGET HIM OR YOUR TRUTHS BECAUSE BETTER SURELY COMES AND WHEN IT DOES COME GIVE HIM GOOD GOD AND ALLELUJAH THANKS. LIFT YOUR HAND AND SPIRIT TO GLORY AND TRULY WALK IN HIS TRUTH; GLORY AND THANKS. So truly listen to this song because wicked people and bad minded people do lurk in the dark whilst praying for you to fall. Some use other means to try and keep you down so that you never rise. But like I've said, keep talking and or praying to Good God and Allelujah because he's your NATURAL MYSTIC THAT CAN AND WILL MOVE EVERY FACET OF EVIL AND WICKEDNESS OUT OF YOUR WAY. Yes this takes time but good have all the time in the world, evil don't. Evil's time is limited to a day, 24 000 years.

Know that life is worth it so let no one tell you otherwise. Do all you can in goodness and truth of you and your surroundings including your good and true family. Grow and guide yourself in good growth because good life does grow; grow up all the time.

Know that in order for you to get somewhere you have to work at it. Blessings take time and so does success. So never give up on your truths despite your trials and tribulations. Never stop talking and or praying to God – Good God and Allelujah like I've said. Your prayer takes time to reach him so continually talk to him. All when yu fed up a trying nuh give up. Give him time and he will hear you. And when he answers you, thank him and do as he says. Know that he Good God and Allelujah will never tell you to steal or kill and or hurt anyone. Your pain and suffering is overbearing I know but hold on. If you can walk and or move away from wicked and evil people pray about it and let Good God move you. If you cannot move tell him you cannot move and let him move your enemy and or enemies perfectly out of the way. Cry to him if you need to cry but never cry bad and or evil for your enemy or enemies. If you do, the bad you pray for for your enemy or enemies will fall back on you. Everyone deserves to live hence pray good at all times.

Absolutely no one can die to see God – Good God and Allelujah hence do not pray in this manner. Do not say, "The Lord is my Sheppard I shall not want." Never ever do this do you hear me. When you say, "the Lord is my Sheppard I shall not want," you are telling him Good God and Allelujah you do not want or need his help nor do you want and need him. Pray in this like manner. "Good God and Allelujah, God of All, Allah and Breath of Life I want and need you. You are my Good Sheppard; All. Please hear my prayer and plea." We truly need him hence we have to acknowledge and receive him. We have to live to see you and the way to do that is by truth. We must live true and clean, good and honest in all that we do in a positive way.

We are to leave negativity alone because evil hath time and it is but for a time before all that is evil dies.

Not one of us was to work hard and kill self for death. You Good God gave us all the tools for success. You gave us all the food including fruit baring trees and herb of the land – earth to maintain and sustain us. We were the ones that wanted more, hence we enslaved each other and kill for what the next man or woman including child has and neglect our own.

You've always been our own but instead of taking care of our own, we gave it up for death and have become death; a part of the dead – the living breathing and walking dead.

There is no life in death so why would I give up my life for death? I want and need to live hence I have to preserve life. I cannot say I truly love my children and readily hand them over to death. I have to secure them and continue to pray good and well for them. Yes if they don't take heed after a while, I am going to leave them alone because they my children do not want or need good for self. Yes I want and need good for you but I cannot do it for you, you have to help self by making the right decisions so that when you have children they too can be saved. All I can do is encourage you and do the good and positive that I can do to help you along your journey so that you succeed. We all have pain and failures in life but it's up to us to pick up the pieces and move on. It's up to us to stay focused and positive. Failures are pluses sometimes because those closed doors are not the doors he Good God and Allelujah want you to go in.

Good God never said kill, he sent his messenger to deliver his message because we cannot hear him nor do we listen. He's given us one last ditched effort to save self because he knew the more we sinned the further into hell we go to die. Meaning instead of spending one nana second in hell and get out billions are stuck there and do die there. Like I've said, each sin has a weight to it and if you have a million sins on your plate and or sin record multiply that sin by each weight, then double your total amount and tack on a bit more time for good measure because death is going to and he can do this. So if one sin is valued at 24000 years in hell double it to 48000 years and if death decides he wants to add another 24000 years on your sentence he can because he's the god of the underworld; death. Hell is his and her domain and death can do whatever he or she damned well please with you in hell. You did not listen to good council on earth; you disobeyed. Death does not have to release you nor will he release you from his grip. These are things the clergy and your parents should have told you but in truth many did not know. And in truth many of you children and young adults refuse to listen. **For many of you money is your game and it matters not how you get the money. As children and young adults many of you don't want to hear and now that time has and** have reached critical mass many of you are going to panic and do more evil things and this is sad. Many of you are going to say, if I had listened. I should have listened and I would not be in this predicament. When we do evil things we cannot undo them. There are no undo buttons to hit for everything to return to normal and be alright again. _As humans we do not think of tomorrow. We live for the here and now in hopes that tomorrow will take care of itself. But tomorrow cannot take care of itself because you determine the outcome of tomorrow, today and the hereafter; your life._

You determine where you go in the grand scheme of things. So if Good God is counselling you for the better, then take the better and put down evil. Know that it's not too late for many hence pray good for you. Meaning talk to Good God and Allelujah truthfully and honestly. Sit up and pray. Stand up and pray but never bow down to the ground that we bury the dead and feces in. This is infinitely and indefinitely forever ever disrespectful. It's an abomination unto Good God and Allelujah so truly don't do it. Lay up in bed, hug your mate in bed and pray whilst holding him or her but never bow down to the _**dirt – earth. Good God and Allelujah is up not down. Death is down hence the downward triangle. The downward triangle represents death so stop bowing down and praying to death. So now you know that when you bow down and pray you are praying to death.**_

He Good God cannot go into hell and rescue you because HE GOOD GOD DOES NOT HAVE THE KEY TO DEATH, DEATH DOES. No, that's not true because he allows his true messengers safe passage via the spirit into hell for us to see what hell and death, even Satan looks like. This is the best way I can explain it because in truth you are not truly in hell you are an observer looking in and seeing what's going on. HE GOOD GOD HAS THE KEY TO LIFE HENCE HE'S BEEN TRYING TO SAVE US AND WE REFUSE TO LISTEN. WE REFUSE TO BE SAVED. WE LET OTHERS TELL US CRAP AND TAKE US OFF OUR GOOD AND TRUE ROAD TO HIM (GOD AND GOOD GOD).

If you know you are on a good path, why leave that good path for unsurity? Keep it.

Why leave the protection and good food of Good God and Allelujah for unclean meat and food including polluted waters of the devil; sin? Come on now.

We say we love but yet have not truth.

We say we love but yet kill life; all life.

We say we love but know not truth or even care for and about truth.

Like I've said, we cannot say we love our children and fuck up their future. That is not love that is hatred. Hence I will forever say; it's the ones that say they love us that fuck up our lives and leave us for dead.

It's the ones that say they love us that hand us over to hell to die.

It's the ones that say they love us that stab us in the back whilst turning the knife a little bit more to ensure that we die; are dead.

It's the ones that say they love us that rape us of our dignity and truth – life and history; heritage.

It's the ones that say they love us that sell us out to the devil and all that is wicked and evil; sinful.

It's the ones that say that they love us that take all from us and leave us starving; wanting of food and water; Good God himself literally.

It's the ones that say they love us that impregnate us and leave us to raise our children by ourselves hence making us single parents. Thus fulfilling the will of evil; the dead. Go back to Genesis of the book of sin; the dead and or your so called holy bible and read about the pain of a woman's childbirth. We were to feel the pain of raising our children alone and this is sad. Yes so said, so done because men were never faithful to their own. They wanted more hence committing adultery over time to fulfill their lustful desires; sexual perversion and needs.

*Know that no child is without a father because he Good God is not dead hence I bug him so to be a father to my children in the living. Now I must bug him about saving their lives in the spiritual realm. I bug him for all future generations forever ever that will share my bloodline, genes and or DNA. All must walk in his righteousness, cleanliness, positivity, truth, honesty, purity infinitely and indefinitely for more than forever ever lifetimes and generations forever ever without end. No sin must come from them. Only truth, honesty, good and true righteousness, good and true as well as honest positivity and purity. They must be infinitely and indefinitely forever ever with end be good and true; positive. They must be true at all times to mother earth and all the goodness she has and have given them. They must keep earth, Mother Earth truly clean and peaceful forever ever without end. Come on now. **I've seen the war and strife; hatred on earth and it must stop; have to stop. Hatred and all evil is negative energy and or of the devil. Hatred is a sin that cuts to the core of man's and or humanities heart. Hatred lead people to kill and***

<u>abuse others and this must stop because God – Good God never said to hate anyone. We are told to separate from evil; all facets of evil and we are the ones to disobey the command and commandments of Good God. One cannot be walking in goodness and have negative energy and or people around them. Things will not work out for you come on now.</u>

Like I've said, I do not hate anyone despite the undertone and the way I write in these books. I refuse to hate you because we are to love each other as we would love ourself. Well I cannot do this love you like I love myself because I do not deal in love, I deal in true love. I refuse to love you. However, I will truly love you.

I refuse to hate you based on societies beliefs of what hate is.

I refuse to give in to evil because evil hath no truth. Nor will I take up arms against you because my words are my weapon and weapons against you. Time and hell is my weapon and weapons against you hence I truly leave the devil and his wicked people to time. What I seek is to separate myself from you and once I do that, you are to stay the hell away from me. This is my true desire and right hence I exercise my right and avoid you. And yes, my spirit will not take certain people and it truly does not take certain people but I do not hate them. Their spirit isn't clean nor do they make positive decisions including some of my children. Hence if I can't take you spiritually I avoid you. Do all to avoid you because I've come to depend on my spirit when it comes to the truth and my spirit is seldom ever wrong. And yes you are trying to avoid someone and your children if you have children take them into your home. At times you will bring that person you are trying to avoid back in your fold due to loneliness but don't be like me, truly avoid them hence avoiding the headaches. Wow the headaches and stress of them; hearing the same old problems over and over again.

Hence true and good goodness is in me for my children and the children and people of him Good God and Allelujah. Hence all is in me, all is around me and all is in me to do good and true, honest and pure; clean and positive will towards all. No, not towards all because all is not from him Good God and Allelujah. Some are of the devil. Hence they give evil everything including war and genetically modified foods.

Know that who Good God has and have ordained man cannot kill because life, true life is given to that person. It is when we leave the fold and folds of Good God and start to walk in sin that we become dead – die. Like I've told you in some of my other books, if he Good God and Allelujah say

Brian sing me a song, you are to continue singing for him until he tells you to stop and or you cannot do it anymore. You are the one to sing his song. You cannot bring anyone else to help you sing because he Good God did not call this person to sing with you, he called you alone hence you alone must travel on your journey with him. It does not mean he will not help you along the way. He will.

Yes you will feel like he does not care but he does. Remember, we live and walk amongst man. Know that the devil and his wicked and evil people are going to pull out every arsenal in their power for you to fail including die, but you can't give up. When you can't take it anymore SCREAM OUT AT THE TOP OF YOUR LUNGS TO HIM GOOD GOD AND ALLELUJAH THAT YOU CANNOT TAKE IT ANYMORE. At times your spirit is going to want to scream like a crazy person, scream because this is what your spirit need. It needs you to scream and cry out to life – Good God and Allelujah for help. Screaming works so truly know what your good spirit is telling you because our spirit has a negative side also. Never listen to the negative side of your spirit. Always listen to the positive side. And yes it's hard to listen to the positive side of you but over time things will become easier. Hence my mandate of November 1, 2014 when it comes to my children. Will this date change? I hope not but somehow I think it will.

When you scream you are not insane you are sane.

I've written what my spirit needs to you. Listen, my spirit can want crazy things at time including a man lying on my back while I write.

At times it wants sex a certain way but I cannot give that which I do not have to give. Meaning I do not have a mate, so I cannot indulge in the exchange of fluids. Hence I have to be contented with what I do not have until he Good God and Allelujah release me,; give me my good and true needs; positive wants and needs that will help us grow up in goodness and in truth. I need him Good God and Allelujah to help me take all negativity and negative energy from me so that I may live in goodness and in truth positively continually without end.

Listen people it's not that I can't go out there and do what my heart and spirit desires. I can but I would be wrong. I would be disrespecting my vow and vows to him Good God and Allelujah and I truly cannot do that. I KNOW THAT WHEN WE ARE WALKING WITH HIM WE CANNOT EXCHANGE FLUIDS WITH A MAN if you do not have a man or woman. You are to keep yourself clean and pure for him, you and humanity; the people he's ordained you to save.

Is it a hard road to travel?

Yes it is but over time it does get better. Some days are harder than some yes but after 7 years of yearning the yearnings dissipate a little. You have to keep going until he sends you the right person if you do not have one. All takes time and we are the ones that are not patient. I'm not but I keep going even when I do wrong. I have to pick myself up and truly do for him because at the end of the day I truly do not want to see anyone go to hell. Nor do I want or need to Good God cry anymore. And you won't comprehend the tears part but I do. His pain is his tears – sufferings. He loves us so but we truly do not love him; can't truly love him. Like I've said time and time again, Good God does not lock anyone out of his abode, we are the ones to lock ourselves out. We are the ones to sin and sin rude and close the doors and windows to him.

Satan and his children did not have to go to hell and die. They had the opportunity to receive Good God and Allelujah and his goodness but because they did not want to give up their sins and sinful ways they chose to go to hell and die. None can blame us for this hence the wickedness of them. Because they are locked out they want all of humanity to be locked out of Good God's kingdom as well and this is wrong on their part. Every human being has a right to live. They also have a chance to redeem self but if you have signed a contract with death you cannot redeem yourself and or self.

These people cannot redeem self because they have their DDC's already. Meaning their name is written in death's book and they have their number – time with death already. All other sins they do is just icing on the cake for death.

❖ *Transgenders*
❖ *Skin Bleachers*

❖ *People that alter self for vanity by having face lifts, nose jobs, butt jobs and or implants, eyebrow lifts etc cannot redeem self. You change self – lie to humanity by saying you look like this when you truly do not. You had help cosmetically.*

❖ *People who commit suicide – this is automatic death.*

❖ *Preachers – clergy for the lies you've told on Good God and Allelujah; Life.*

❖ *Disobedient children that disobey Good God and Allelujah – this is automatic death. See Eve of your book of Genesis.*

❖ *Satanist*
❖ *Illuminati's*

❖ *Voodoo Priests and Priestess*
❖ *Obeah Workers of iniquity amongst others cannot redeem self. You are hell bound. No not hell bound because your containment unit of fire awaits you upon your death literally. This cannot change because it is so. Thus saith the Lord thy God meaning it is so.*

CHANGE THE DIRTY LINEN OF SELF AND SEE THE BEAUTY OF HIM GOOD GOD AND ALLELUJAH COME ON NOW.

No one told you to sin but you did anyway. You know your father is wrong, don't carry on the tradition and go to hell with him. Change for the better and put down dirty traditions because they cannot save you, they can only kill you.

Traditions of men are not traditions of God; Good God and Allelujah come on now. Stop teaching your children wrong. Good God and Allelujah have no tradition or traditions. Life is not a tradition, it is our right and it's wrong for anyone to take this right from you. Come on now.

Stop teaching others wrong.

Stop teaching self wrong and stop lying to yourself because at the end of the day, lies do deceive; kill. Good God gave you life, take care of it as well as take care of your children's life if you have kids and or children.

Why sacrifice them to death if you can give them true life. Many of us cook and see the boiling water in the pot. So why would you want to give this boiling water to your child knowing how deadly this water is? This is death, so why give it to your child? Come on now. Why would you want them to burn in this boiling water? If this boiling water can burn you and leave you scared even kill you; what say you when it comes to the fire of hell and your spirit?

Now tell me something, is this warranted for you or anyone?

No right?

So why let someone do this to you, send you to hell to burn worse than this?

More importantly, why give it to your child and or children and Good God?

Death is not warranted but yet we justify it. How can you justify death?

No death is justified, not even suicide.

Once a person commits suicide there is no way in hell they can retrieve their soul and or spirit from death; hell. Not even your goodness can help them because they are truly gone. Meaning if there was a saving grace in the grave for us he or she who have taken their life in the living would get none. To take your own life is automatic death, meaning upon your spirit leaving your body and or flesh you go straight to hell. Your soul and or spirit goes directly to hell. Hence many can see the fire that burns them literally. So when the clergy tell you bullshit of someone saving you in the grave tell them I say to kiss your ass because not all is saved and or will be saved. This they should know if they are of God – Good God and Allelujah; Life.

When we give up our lives for death, WE ARE GIVING UP OUR PLACE WITH GOOD GOD AND ALLELUJAH. We are literally telling him Good God and Allelujah that we do not want or need a place with him. We don't want or need him because we have someone else already.

It matters not what the other man or religion say. Good God will infinitely and indefinitely never ever tell you to sin or go against his words. His word is his word and it's not right nor is it just for anyone to tell you to disobey him. This is why I tell you, I will never ever tell anyone to choose my god because we are to know THAT HE GOOD GOD AND ALLELUJAH IS THE TRUTH. HE GAVE US ALL THAT IS GOOD AND TRUE AND WE ARE THE ONES TO THROW IT AWAY.

WE ARE THE ONES TO HATE AND OR PUT STRIFE BETWEEN US AND THE NEXT PERSON; NATION.

WE ARE THE ONES TO HATE BASED ON RELIGION.

WE ARE THE ONES TO HATE BASED ON HUE – SKIN COLOUR.

WE ARE THE ONE TO HATE BASED ON EYE COLOUR.

WE ARE THE ONES TO HATE BASED ON RELIGIOUS AFFILIATION.

WE ARE THE ONES TO HATE BECAUSE YOUR FRIEND DON'T LIKE THE NEXT MAN AND OR COUNTRY.

WE ARE THE ONES TO HATE BASED ON TRADITIONS OF MEN.

WE ARE THE ONES TO HATE BECAUSE SOMEONE TELL US TO.

All we do to displease and dishonour self and god. Come on now.

Good God specifically gave us life and we told him unconditionally that we do not want it. We told him unconditionally that sin is worth it hence we sin and die. We continuously sin without thinking of the consequences and this is wrong because "the wages (pay) of sin is death." We know this but yet sin anyway.

We have children and gave them over to sin without thinking of the consequences, the fire of hell that is going to burn and char that little child.

We are the ones that gave our children over to a lifetime of suffering and pain in hell. We cannot take pain and suffering but yet we are expecting our children to take it. Your responsibility as a parent is to protect that child and if you cannot protect and or take care of that child you will be held at fault, responsible and accountable for the lack of life's necessities; parenting. You did not provide for that child hence you will be held guilty of sin and be charged with sin. We are the keepers of life hence we are to keep life; guard life and protect life.

We are to maintain and sustain life just as Mother Earth (Physical) and Father God (Spiritual) has and have maintained and sustained us all. Know this. We are our brothers and sisters keepers but not all our brothers and sisters want good keeping; good housekeeping.

If you know you cannot take on the responsibility of raising a child do not have

one nor let a man force you to have one. It is a sin BECAUSE HE TOO WILL BE CHARGED FOR CHILD ABANDONMENT.

HE TOO WILL BE CHARGED FOR NEGLECT AND HE WILL BE FOUND GUILTY AND HELD ACCOUNTABLE FOR SIN. And this is what's happened to the clergy and many parents globally. Many take on a responsibility as keepers of Good God's children but instead of keeping Good God's house they taint and dirty it. They were not true hence they preach and teach falsely whilst sending themselves further into hell to die.

It takes two to raise a child hence he Good God never truly left us by ourselves. Mother God has always been around to help us and whether we like it or not she has always been Earth, earthly. Hence the female God humanity has on earth. We are the ones that don't take care of her. No we are not to worship and or bow down to earth, we are to keep her clean and true to us. She gave to us good and clean and we are the ones to give to her dirty and unclean.

As parents and youths; young adults we are to do good and live clean. When we have our children we are to raise them good and clean and in the good and clean manner of Good God and Allelujah.

Like I've said before in my other books, we are the ones that do not ask Good God and Allelujah for good and clean, honest and righteous, pure and true as well as positive children. So because of this, some of us have to be constantly praying and talking to God and asking him to protect our children so that they do not take the folly ground or walk the folly ground.

It's not easy hence tell him and bug him Good God and Allelujah for future generations that share my Genes and or DNA to be pure, upright, just, clean, honest, truthful, righteous children that will not walk in the way of evil indefinitely without end forever ever. Even when we forget to ask him for this I need him to bless us with upright, clean and just, pure and positive, honest and truthful children that will never ever walk in the way of evil. Do this if you don't have children and want children. When you have your children teach them to trust God – Good God and Allelujah.

Teach them to ask him (Good God and Allelujah) for honest and clean, pure and righteous children that will never ever leave him nor walk in the way of the wicked and evil from a young age. Teach them to do all that is positive and not evil. Establish a good and true bond with them, you and Good God and let this bond be forever ever without end. Trust me if I could go back in time and ask Good God for this knowing what I know now, I would not hesitate, I would go back in time quicker than you could say amen.

You have the way of Good God and Allelujah now so teach your children right. Remember we made a vow to him, so why can't we honour our vow to him?

Why can't we be truthful to him?

You alone can change the dirty linen off you so do it. Wash yourself clean and become clean. For billions of you it's too late but if you are with God – Good God and Allelujah you will never be too late. Yes for some true friends and family that truly loves you can save you, so help them to help you so that you are saved.

The door is not fully closed even though I saw a full charcoal black moon. You have a chance to save self and family; your true loved ones so do it.

You know death comes on a massive scale before 2032 so do all you can to save you and your family – children. As parents it's not right to watch our children die because death was never ordained for anyone. Your child and or children should be a part of your life because in many ways they are extensions of us; you. We felt the pain in raising them as well as bring them into this world and you have to protect them from the evils of this world. You as a parent and or adult cannot let your sins and or generational sins continue to fall on them (our children); you. They need saving as well and if we cannot save them and or teach them to save self, how are they going to? It's not fair to them nor is it fair to you because at the end of the day, it's your life and their life. **Hell is not nice because it's hot and we've forgotten this. To be honest with you, I truly don't know why anyone would choose hell; death over life.**

Truly take a good look at the earth and all the lands of the earth. Many of us vacation in other lands and we see the beauty of these vacation properties. So if we like these vacation properties and their beauty why give it up for hell; death?

All this beauty you see on earth you are definitely not going to see in hell so why send you there?

Why send your child there?

Some of us have so much heartache on earth raising our children; why want to die and go

to hell to face hardships worse than you are facing on earth?

And no Jasmine hell is not better because when you can call up your enemy and or girlfriend and cuss them out via Skype, Twitter, Cellular, home phone, email and or a letter, you cannot do this in hell. Your home is just a cubby hole with fire that burns your spirit. You are going to want water and none will be given to you. And if you do get water it's boiling water that you are going to get. Remember Jesus and the cross how he wanted water and the demons; wicked people of hell gave him vinegar to drink? Well this is you in hell. The demons of hell will give you water, but the water they give up is boiling water. 100 Degrees Celsius is the boiling point of water; well the water of hell is infinitely and indefinitely hotter than 360 degrees Celsius and lava combined. Your child and or children is going to want water and none will be given to them except for this boiling water.

Let's put it this way. You believe Jesus was crucified on a cross and we've seen movies depicting this. Think of you in hell dying over and over again in this like manner if not worse. I've told you, the demons of hell live to inflict pain. Pain to them is like the best sex you've ever had. Pain is their sex. So truly know what side you are on as well as the side you've chosen for your child and or children.

Yes the children of today are not listening nor do they hear. Remember we too were where they are now. How many of us listened to our parents when we were younger?

How many of us listen to good council when we were younger?

Some of us our parents told us not to have a man (Boyfriend) but behind their backs we had our little hock on the side that we saw after school or in the park.

Some of us lied by saying we were going to the library and before we knew it, we were in his arms at his house and or someplace.

The game is there with our children and many of us know them but turn a blind to it when it comes to our children.

Like many of you, we try to shelter our children and we have to stop doing this. Evil is there and they know it. Some are influenced by friends hence none of us can run from evil. Evil is everywhere and it's a shame. Go back to the time of Noah because every race have 6000 years to do good; change and if we refuse good then death comes on a massive scale. That massive scale is here today and it's sad but this is the choice we made. Yes the Europeans have their chance to choose. It's their shot to accept life and or reject it. I cannot choose for them because that choice is not for me to make. They can accept these words or reject them but it's up to them and not me. Nor is it up to Good God and Allelujah to choose for them.

Is my job done?

I truly hope not because despite my dream of the death I have hope and trust in Good God and Allelujah.

The dream: I saw Babylonians – a mixture of Black and Indian; more like Somalian in feature. They were Muslim. They had this sliver gray and shinny line. More like a fishing line cast for me. But I did not fall in their trap. This silver gray line is death. This silver gray shiny line is like unto the line I told you about in another book with the airplane going up and coming down.

This line I saw in Toronto, around the Albion and Tandridge region in Rexdale. So I am not sure if somewhere in Toronto is going to get bombed and or someone is going to get killed by Islam extremist. I say extremist because like I said, these people cry Allah but take away from the breath of life (Allah) with the killing that they do. They say life but death and murder is in their hearts. They are not of Good God and Allelujah hence they take life at all costs. GOOD GOD HAS WARNED HIS PEOPLE; THE JEWS ABOUT THEM (THE ISLAMIC KINGDOM AND WORLD) AND IF THEY DON'T TAKE HEED THEY WILL BE LEFT BEHIND TO THE DEATH THAT THEY CHOSE. Islam and Christianity is death. They preach and teach death hence they are the same and not of God; Good God. So to the Jews that walk in the way of Islam by marrying into this fold, tomorrow comes for your asses because you have to answer to God. So truly good luck to many of you that have abandoned your truth; God.

I also saw a plane go up (take off) and come down. But before the plane could crash it went back up in the air. So the plane did not crash. This I saw in the southeastwardly direction of Downsview Park. Southeastwardly is the best way to describe the direction.

Funny in the dream I was speaking to someone I knew Venezuelan. She was dark and darkness was around her. She was telling me God was going to make me fly. We were on the balcony of the building I live in. It's so weird because before she told me God was going to make me fly, I almost fell off the balcony but I caught myself.

So I don't know if the plane falling and going back up is in Venezuela or another South American and or Spanish land. So South America and or Spanish lands start doing thorough maintenance checks of your fleet of planes. You are being warned because I take this as a dream in dream.

It's August 29, 2014 and the weird dreams are coming. Just this morning I dreamt I was in Jamaica at my uncle's house but it was not my uncle's house. I was looking outside and I could see the wind gusting and blowing hard. The wind was blowing at the mango trees that had partially ripe mangoes on them. A lot of mangoes were on the tree and I could see two apes and or monkey's playing in the tree. The wind did them nothing but they were in the mango tree. I did not want them to get all the mangoes and I wanted to go into the wind to get some of the mangoes but I did not. I stayed inside the house that was affected by the wind. I did not see my little cousin and I was wondering what happened to him but was told he was working for which I found odd. This little boy, about 3 – 5 years of age was in the house and it was as if he was my cousin's son. My cousin is male and is almost 18 years old people so this was odd to me that he had a son this old. Like I said, the house was not solid because a cup filled with tea was on the table and it shifted as if to overturn and spill but it did not spill. The cup just ran across the table. Yes this is a weird dream for me because monkey's in a tree filled with mangoes is a first for me I think. So if any of you have a clue what this dream means truly let me know. I so do not know if a hurricane is going to touch down in Jamaica without causing damage or what but who knows? Yes I kinda have a clue as to the meaning of this dream but I am so not sure.

For all who want to reach me or follow me can do so on Twitter. My Twitter address is MichelleJean77. I rarely use it, meaning tweet.

*I've set up an email address for my books at <u>Michellejeanbooks@gmail.com</u>. Feel free to send me a email, but if you send death threats, spam, racist comments, obscene pictures, viruses and or anything of this nature including all I've not mentioned, you will truly not like how I respond. Keep your hate mail to yourself because my head is hot. I will take on your racism and the way I rinse out your wat nat clate Good God himself will not like it. He will hold his head down in shame. Hence you are duly warned. Yes you are entitled to your freedom of speech and so am I. <u>**Hence if you LIVE IN A GLASS HOUSE TRULY DO NOT THROW STONES. WE JAMAICANS DON'T JUST THROW BACK WE TUMBLE DOWN.**</u> So if you cannot take the heat do not walk the borders of hell and or go into hell with me because* *you will get burned brutally with my words and or the way I answer you.*

If you don't want the fire blazing truly don't start anything by lighting it and or adding fuel to a dormant volcano and that volcano is me.

Billions will not like me and will seek my hurt but I say to you, invest your energy in truth not negativity; evil.

Hell is there and if you don't want to go there truly live right and not wrong.

We say civility but we're not civilized beings. We live to hate and do hate; kill. Yes we all have a right to live but when Judas's of the world come around you have to do all that is good to pull away from them.

We all say God but instead of striving to see God in a good and true way, we follow others and die; go to hell. This is your life and my life and how dare you want to take that from me. You say your God say kill and steal and you will go directly to paradise. Well your god is a fucking liar, murderer and thief. Why the fuck would I leave my Good God of peace and truth for your demented demon of wickedness of a God; yours. Why should I defile him to become ugly and sinful like you? Come on now.

All when unnu tek mi bady, mi still a go bi loyal to my God because I know where I'm from and where I am going with him. He's life and when your ass is burning in hell I am relaxing with feet (spirit) up enjoying him and all the pleasures he's given me in his world. I'm not the one in hell burning like a bitch you are. Hence I am blessed and highly favoured. Stay in hell because I know the kingdom of God; Good God and Allelujah do not have many people. All who say they were of him or for him backstabbed him and became disloyal and I refuse to be like any of you; them.

Keep your god but say the fuck away from mine because he's mine and not yours. Your god is death so continue praising death. Don't want or need anything from my God and True Friend; Life.

Do my children know the truth? They do because they know something bad is going to happen in humanity shortly. I don't have to tell them this. They can feel it hence I hear them talking about it to their friends. No not all talk about it because not all know. But my first two talks about it. They are just waiting for the bad to happen. They know so what say you; the rest of humanity including children.

Michelle Jean

Musical Notes

I've been listening to a variety of music lately and I have to say I am amazed at how great some of these artists are, but yet you cannot find their music in the mainstream; daily radio rotation. Hence I wrote this to Good God and Allelujah.

It is so weird Good God. I've been listening to Rueben Studdard Unconditional Love and If I Could Give You the World with Lalah Hathaway. But call me crazy because you know my brain doesn't work normally hence these words to you.

It's weird how we say we love you but can't sing songs like these to you. Write songs of beauty like these to you.

We say we love you but can't dedicate truth to you.

We cry out to you and beg you for everything including a saving grace from hell but when it comes to truly giving you and singing songs of truth like these to you we can't do it.

We say you are our father but in all we do and have done is disrespect you and cause you shame and pain.

Right now I am so confused; thinking I am the crazy one but why can't we dedicate goodness and truth to you also? Are you not our unconditional love? So if you are; why can't we give you the world in goodness and in truth?

Why can't we reserve time for you? I mean we pray but is that truly reserving time for you?

How about a dinner date with just you? Maybe a dance or two; that candle light dinner for two.

How about just buying you a rose and setting it on our table and say God, Good God and Allelujah; Allah this is for you?

It's like we have our wives and husbands including girlfriends and children but I've never heard anyone say you are their rose and if they could give you the world they would. All we do is bitch and complain about our sorrows and pain. But what about your sorrows and pain? What about your life?

This gentleman (Rueben Studdard) has touched a chord with me with these songs. They get me thinking about you and your feelings. You're not dead, you're alive but yet we can't dedicate beautiful songs like these to you.

Yes I get down on you but I have to truly think because life is worth living with you and for you.

There is true beauty in you and I know this beauty can't be explained at times but we are not the only ones in this relationship; you are in it too. So why can't we truly love you and dedicate true love songs to you?

I know many of us can't see you but if we truly open our eyes and hearts we can see you in your true state over time.

God - Good God and Allelujah why can't this be with us? I want to dedicate these songs to you but I can't because these songs are you and I truly, more than truly love you unconditionally and you know this.

Life isn't about being ashamed of the person you are with or even being ashamed of you Good God. Life is about truth and true love. And if you cannot love that person true and accept them for who they are then you cannot truly love nor do you truly love them. Neither can you love you true because you are flawed; the flawed one.

We put others in brackets and categories and this is wrong. It's like if you are a size 20, I don't want you because you are too fat, you need to be skinny and have the shape of a super model. We set unrealistic

BLACKMAN REDEMPTION – THE YOUTHS

goals for people and when you cannot achieve these goals you are fat and ugly. Come on now, why can't I truly be me? Why do I have to be what you want me to be? Is it not my life? So why am I letting you live it for me and or tell me how to live and what to do?

Am I daft and or stupid that I need you to dominate and control me? I truly love me and I will not change to please and suit you? This package, my package is perfect with me and my maker, so why should you have a problem with it; my package?

I truly don't know Good God. We all want perfection but truly do not see that we are perfect the way we are. Stop trying to change me because you are not more beautiful than me. I do not need to be a size 2 or 12. I need to truly be me. And if you are not alright with this; me, then leave me alone and don't comment about me. I am happy being me. You are not happy being you because you buy beauty;

friends I don't. Hence you notice me and tell me that I am the flawed one when you are the flawed one. You cannot see true beauty. All you can see is vanity; hence you buy vanity to make yourself look ugly, wanting and needy.

Good God, true love is attainable no matter the rareness of it. I attained true love and beyond with you but with all this said; I cannot show humanity this. I cannot touch them and let them feel what I am talking about.

This love doesn't hurt Lovey because it cannot be conceived by humanity; meaning they cannot comprehend it. It's like creating a whole new universe that is so light and bright it can be seen in time by the human eye. Nothing is hidden because all is done with truth, true and unconditional love.

Oh Lovey if only. Truly if only because humanity would feel no pain or sorrow if I had my own way with you.

You Lovey; Good God and Allelujah would feel no pain or sorrow but yet I know on the days my feelings overflow like a river you feel no pain or sorrow; just joy and happiness. I know you hold your head high and proud knowing at least one truly loves you more than unconditionally without end.

Enjoy my father, my true love, my life and all. Truly enjoy. You are mother and father and I will never forget you. Nor will I forget my biological mother that you gave me because I truly thank you for her as well as truly love her unconditionally.

Michelle
August 20, 2014

Ah Good God there is a sense of disappointment in me today. All these things I need to do but cannot do it with you, why?

I want to walk with you on the Blue Mountain hand in hand but can't.

I want to talk to you face to face in the flesh but can't.

I want to sing beautiful ballads of praise to you but can't. Hence I will write them, write songs of praise unto to you real soon.

I will write songs of truth and unconditional love to you because I truly need to let the world know and feel my truth towards you and for you.

I will anoint you with songs and make everything in your world be truly alright. Not just for you and me but for humanity also.

In all you've done, you've been so giving; true and it's unfortunate as humans in humanity, we cannot see this nor can we hold you although we are married to you. We are your bond and you are our bond of truth and true love but none of us can see this.

Our marriage and or bond is sacred hence we are to love you true.

You are our guide and protector; provider and healer.

How great and wonderful it would be if we could do all this Good God and truly put down hate - strife.

How great and wonderful it would be if we could all come fully clean and void of all sins - sinful things.

Good God wouldn't it be wonderful. I mean if humans could feel your truth and true love like I do?

Wouldn't it be great if we could walk and live together in unity and true peace?

Oh Good God maybe one day you will truly bless me an let me find true love within more than I have now.

Maybe one day you will bless me and hold my hand, walk with me and tell me Michelle everything is okay between me and you. Fear not nor fair anything because you are with me and will always be with me forever ever infinitely and indefinitely without end.

Michelle
August 21, 2014

*We all sing just a closer walk with thee,
just a closer walk with thee; but Good God
and Allelujah why can't we hold your
hand too?*

*Why can't we be comforted just thinking of
you and only you?*

*It's great walking with thee but yet we do
not know that true love cannot end. It is
constantly and constantly grows up; glow.*

*Ah Lovey meet me on the Blue Mountain
soon so that we can walk and talk hand
in hand together in truth; harmony. We
could even have dinner; drink a glass of
wine or two.*

*Ah Good God and Lovey, man cannot
make our wine only you.*

*Know that you are my darling and
friend, true keep in good and bad times.
You are my comforter; comforter of joy
and not sorrow.*

Yes problems come but they also go.
We will solve them together peacefully and truthfully.

I truly miss you. Miss having you to hold.

Miss having you say, Michelle I truly love you.

I miss all about you hence Return; truly come back home in a positive and true way.

You are truly my keep hence I have to truly keep you and abide by you and with you.

You are my bestest of friend; my sunshine throughout the day.

You are endless because you are more than endless love; you are my one true love.

Michelle Jean
August 21, 2014

Good God let me sing to you.

I crave you; yearn you. So let me truly be there for you and sing you ballads of praise; true beauty and joy.

How good and wonderful if you could walk and talk man - humanity once again; with me.

Ah Lovey plant a true in your goodness and truth; true love for me.

Plant your heavenly and pure, positive and good; perfect tree for me, with me and in me.

Give me a sign Good God and Lovey that you've done this and that you are truly with me; more than protective of me all the time.

Lovey it's morning time, won't you have breakfast with me?

Be that face, my beautiful and perfect shining star at my table that I look upon with glee - pride; and a beautiful warm and pleasant smile. Ah my darling you are my true hope - cause. You are my cause and effect, my songs of true love and joy; praise.

Lovey be truly happy with me on this day; every day for that matter.

Let nothing come between us and let our true love never ever fade.

Take my hand, dance with me in the morning dew. Light up your face because your smile is my smile. Your smile is more beautiful than anything I've ever known. Yes I know the sun is bright, hot but you are not the sun, you are so much more. You are infinitely sweeter, warmer, tender; meek and mild hence the sun has nothing on you when it comes to the true warmth of me and you.

Michelle Jean
August 21, 2014

So as I close this book, here are a few artist I found on the internet that did something for me and or wowed me with their voice.

Jamiel   Real Father
Christopher Martin   Just Like You

Nature   Revolution &
Trying Man - these songs bring tears to my eyes to know that this is how some of our people are living globally and the politicians of the land let things like this happen. They care not for their own hence I plea and plead with Good God and Allelujah to never ever open his door to a politician of wickedness and heartlessness. I truly have no sympathy for them because to me a politician that allows their people to suffer is heartless and without a heart. Hence I pray no mercy for them and their children; family. I will however, pray that he Good God and Allelujah see the needs of the people of the land and truly help them out of their sufferation and or situations.

Many of us are trying people; hence we do what we can to make ends meet. Our efforts; trying and trust in God - Good God is all we have hence we keep going until better comes. Yes who feels it knows it. That's why we keep walking until we cannot walk anymore; we sit down and rest until another day comes when we get up and walk again; trying, selling, singing, praising, dancing, talking, handing out flyers. Hope is ours hence hope is never lost. It's with us hence we keep it forever ever without end. Today is yours but tomorrow, the beauty of tomorrow is mine and it's in me hence the truth and the truth of God - Good God and Allelujah is in me to keep and I keep him always.

Uncle Jed
Josh Krajcik
Sam Bailey
Will Perrett
Attraction (Interpretive dance group)
Bugle   Divine Intervention

Wyre featuring Alaine   Nakupenda Pia
Kidis ft DNA, Ameleena, Wyre   Twajichanganya
(Kamua Leo)

Syd ft I T   Replay   -
Somehow this video reminds me of Sean
Kingston

Syd featuring Wyre   Guardian Angel

Diamond   Mbagala
Diamond   Mawazo
Diamond   Kesho

Dr. Jose Chameleone   Wale Wale
Dr. Jose Chameleone   Badilisha
Dr. Jose Chameleone   Valu Valu
Dr. Jose Chameleone   Calling Me

Radio & Weasel   NKWETAGA
(African Dancehall)

OTHER BOOKS BY MICHELLE JEAN

Blackman Redemption – The Fall of Michelle Jean
Blackman Redemption – After the Fall Apology
Blackman Redemption – World Cry – Christine Lewis
Blackman Redemption
Blackman Redemption – The Rise and Fall of Jamaica
Blackman Redemption – The War of Israel
Blackman Redemption – The Way I Speak to God
Blackman Redemption – A Little Talk With Man
Blackman Redemption – The Den of Thieves
Blackman Redemption – The Death of Jamaica
Blackman Redemption – Happy Mother's Day
Blackman Redemption – The Death of Faith
Blackman Redemption – The War of Religion
Blackman Redemption – The Death of Russia
Blackman Redemption – The Truth
Blackman Redemption – Spiritual War

The New Book of Life
The New Book of Life – A Cry For The Children
The New Book of Life – Judgement
The New Book of Life – Love Bound
The New Book of Life – Me
The New Book of Life – Life

Just One of Those Days
Book Two – Just One of Those Days
Just One of Those Days – Book Three The Way I Feel
Just One of Those Days – Book Four

The Days I Am Weak
Crazy Thoughts – My Book of Sin

Broken
Ode to Mr. Dean Fraser

A Little Little Talk
A Little Little Talk – Book Two

Prayers
My Collective
A Little Talk/A Time For Fun and Play
Simple Poems
Behind The Scars
Songs of Praise And Love

Love Bound
Love Bound – Book Two

Dedication Unto My Kids
More Talk
Saving America From A Woman's Perspective
My Collective the Other Side of Me
My Collective the Dark Side of Me
A Blessed Day
Lose To Win
My Doubtful Days – Book One

My Little Talk With God
My Little Talk With God – Book Two

A Different Mood and World – Thinking

My Nagging Day
My Nagging Day – Book Two

Friday September 13, 2013
My True Love
It Would Be You
My Day

A Little Advice – Talk
1313, 2032, 2132 – The End of Man
Tata

MICHELLE'S BOOK BLOG – BOOKS 1 – 18

My Problem Day
A Better Way
Stay – Adultery and the Weight of Sin – Cleanliness
Message

Let's Talk
Lonely Days – Foundation
A Little Talk With Jamaica – As Long As I Live
Instructions For Death